The Bedside Guide
to No Tell Motel
Second Floor

The Bedside Guide to No Tell Motel
Second Floor

Edited by

Reb Livingston & Molly Arden

No Tell Books 2007
Reston, VA

No Tell Books - http://www.notellbooks.org

Cover Design: Sonya Naumann

Proofreader: Joseph Massey

ISBN: 978-0-6151-6437-3

in fond memory of kari edwards

Contents

Core of Affections

The Difference Between Slutty and Sexy

May Be Just Shy of a Half of a Cunt Hair, reports Molly Arden:

When Molly Arden undertakes the arduous task of pinning down the subtleties between the vulgar and the salacious she finds herself at odds.

What does it matter the difference between safe sex every Sunday night with the same old stiff and hardcore *"Get Wet Girls"* pleasuring themselves with lollypops? Does the do-er make the difference when deciphering the difference in sexy and slutty? Is it in the intention? Is it audience? Is it possible that the same pole dance performed in front of a group of businessmen, tipsy on Slippery Nipples, is not the same dance if performed in the safety of a bedroom to an audience of one? Is it the comfortable shelter of a mature relationship that allows for the delicate web of sexy to weave itself loosely around a couple like warm yarn?

Can a slutty vixen tempt a hot Rod towards the loving confines of a long term relationship? Does the don of a long term relationship mean the virtual extinction of smutty, raunchy love? We've all seen that married couple still slapping asses in the frozen food aisle at the Whole Foods, or pulling bites off each other's forks with wet lips that are familiar and yet pouty with interest. They are sexy. They have sex and pay bills and wash their sheets regularly and retire in sleepwear that is comfortable and functional. Smuty? Raunchy? Maybe that depends on the night.

It's an easier task to spot those things that are simply UNsexy. Women with cracked heels and terrible feet are not sexy. Men with fleshy hips and pants hiked above their navels are not sexy. Nipple hairs on women are never sexy. Neither is dandruff. I could go on for days. And where the fuck has sexy been that Justin Timberlake had to be dispatched to bring it back? Maybe it crossed the line, went to visit its sister—the darker, more lurid dirty girl: raunch. Molly has, in her day, run with the stickier, uglier of these two sisters, and although on the surface she's the less popular one, the sluttier, more stickier can always be counted on to be a sure thing. Her bed's always sticky, worn to shreds, then abandoned for other places with better angles, different heights. Because it is so vulgar, so terrifying in the light, the very soul of raunch depends upon discretion—plain paper wrapping, false names, hourly rates, and love letters written on skin and safely eaten. Without the need to woo, there's anonymity for some and, for others, a need to claim her like a discounted Burberry coat at Filenes's Basement you can't believe has gone unnoticed.

For Some Reason I'm Compelled to Note: We're Not Smut Peddlars, reports Reb Livingston:

Amen Molly. While promoting the first *Bedside Guide*, I encountered a number of strange ideas regarding the concept of *sexy*, as well as poetry. One encounter was with a reporter from a news wire service who assumed by the book's title the poems were about adultery. Although disappointed when I explained the premise, he still wrote the 150 word piece which had very little to do with the book (which he did not read), instead presented Molly and me as "experts in the art of seductive poetry" who advised against rhyming "cock" with "rock." While amused, we weren't entirely comfortable with our new *expert* status, nonetheless we appreciated the press and the piece resulted in an on-air interview with an Irish radio station. Unfortunately the interview didn't go so well. The host asked, "My friend's name is Mary—what should one rhyme with that?" My response, "Avoid rhyming anything with her name." The host considered that unsatisfactory and pressed for a better answer. All I could come up with was an uninspired "cherry." Bleh. Then I read a poem from the book, a dreamy, lush, romantic poem that ended with kissing, one of my favorites. The host said she wasn't seduced one bit, cut the interview short and that was that. Perhaps a more seductive ditty would have went like:

Oh darling take stock
it's off with my frock
and on to your cock

I don't consider the above sexy and can't imagine anyone over the age of 12 who might be turned on by such. But to varying degrees, many people expected that from the first *Bedside Guide* and likely our racy cover and tongue-in-cheek marketing contributed to such expectations. For the sake of clarity for this volume: **We are not smut peddlers. This is not a collection of dirty ditties.**

If you think panty-free celebrities flashing their genitalia to the paparazzi is hot, well God bless and bully for you, you're living in the right decade—but you will not find poems describing such in this book. Not that these poems ignore the delectable sensuality of flesh. You'll find plenty ruminating on body and touch. But that is one layer of sexy, one form of intimacy, and these poems do not limit themselves to such. As humans we desire many things from one another, from and for our bodies, our minds and yes, our souls, especially our gasping, suffering souls. We desire connections, we desire to be noticed, we desire to be near, to be understood, to be considered, to be admired and to be remembered. Desire can be titillating and thrilling. It can also be tender, strained, conflicted, solemn, sad, angry and disappointing. Desire can sometimes be reciprocated, appreciated, unheard, rebuffed, squandered and taken for granted. Desire can be joyful, surprising, painful, bleak or outright menacing. Desire can be a gift, a chore or a curse. What we desire, what we crave, what turns us on, is what we find appealing, our own private sexy.

What I find most captivating about these poems are their ranges of passions and where these passions lead. Some of these places are unexpected, some a little awkward and weird. In some cases these are dark, vulnerable or somber places, not what our current popular culture is currently associating with sexy. But these are poems, something long expunged from popular culture, so we feel no urge to venture down that over-tramped path. No sloppy seconds offered here.

Anatomy of Mortals

Nicole Steinberg

Fortune

If a girl tells you to eat something
off her tits, you'd better do it.
Even if it's sardines, you will do it.

Laurel K. Dodge

I Will Bake You Cookies and You Will Eat Them

I'll put on my Jackie O's,
the better for you to not see me.
I'll cinch an apron around
my waist. There'll be no mistaking
what I'm trying to be: Woman-
ly. I'll whip up a batch of saffron
cookies, the color of which
will remind you of piss
and your real country.
How many precious threads
must be steeped before the dough
goes urine in my hands?
My baked goods will be crisp
between your teeth.
I will never admit to your arrogant
chin that your vicious
grin reminds me of the moon
in the middle of the night, that unforgiving
son of a bitch. When you're dead,
there'll still be a cutting
edge to that whiteness.
Whoever digs up your remains
will wonder: Was he ever happy?
But there'll be no skeleton.
Your ashes will blow like dried
stigmas into the river, an ingredient
to be incorporated. Mother
will welcome you with muddy
arms. When baking, one must follow
the recipe exactly. If I'm alive,
if I survive you, allow me to touch

Laurel K. Dodge

the flame to your dear head.
My hands will shake. I'll nearly throw up
from the excitement. At last,
husband, we will be married.

23

David Lehman

Tit wears a scarf...

Tit wears a scarf,
Cock wears a hat,
Belly is flat,
Ass curves phat.

Balls are in their sack,
Ankles in their sandals,
Hair down her back,
Eyes replace candles.

Cock tips his fedora,
Says hi to Dolores.
Tit wears a scarf.
Curls surround clitoris.

Pussy wears the flora
And fauna of the deep.
Eyes will not weep
When flesh falls asleep.

Noah Falck

from Life As a Crossword Puzzle

5. Across

My mustache is mechanical.
When I smile it knows of no happiness.

My mustache of fame. My mustache of fortune.

There is a tale that speaks of a mustache
that waits to become something else,
perhaps a beard.

The 1970's were overgrown with mustaches.

As a boy I studied the exactness of Rollie Finger's mustache.
The pitcher with the knuckleball
and the mustache.

1977: the embarrassing legend of everyone's mustache.

She says my mustache exfoliates her back.
She is seduced within the tickle arena of mustache hair.

Melt your ice cream in the mustache of sunlight.

"Our mustaches are all we have."

The gym teacher wore a mustache.
She was laughed at behind closed doors.
She knew this, but also knew the powers of the mustache.

Piotr Gwiazda

First Date

I'm clipping my nails.
You're shaving your legs.

We're going to have sex
and we know it.

Salwa C. Jabado

After the sex

my smoothed over breasts
eye me like plaintive fish
swimming, doubling back,
flitting briefly in the mirror
as I bend to fill a glass of water
in the sink.
Straightening up
my waist appears
cinched and saddle high
a v on either side
delineating the well-handled
masa-bowl of my belly.
Happily disbelieving
transformations,
I turn out the light,
sending fish and flesh to bed.

Molly Needs a Hand

In a tub, the delicate triangle
of fingers and book,
the other hand dry to turn pages.

Is there freedom, as early Christians
or recent Christinas say, in submersion?

She needs you to lend a hand
not just fingers but your whole hand.
The whole great meat thing of it.

Take it off and give it to her.

I know what you're thinking.
You're thinking that I am she.
I'm not responsible for those thoughts.

A cunt with less appetite
and no imagination
might chew or suck
or even fuck it in desperation
where "it" stands for the hand
Molly wants to borrow from you
so she can ease with mirth
into the pleasures of her bath.

You can watch—but only if you agree
to give a big hand when she sighs
in the satisfaction of your eyes.

The hand is a scribe. The hand will write
your fate in fog on the bathroom mirror.

Sarcophagus: To the bed

amounts to porchlight. The sidewalk
muddled through his hair. Our weapon is these: my this
on his, his this on this like a marriage not stretched out as Tennessee
but more

the notch Ohio is. Near
a pond superfluous
with cod. *These.* Nearer me, he never mouths open

at morning. For the breath
secure as a bench
my tongue could sit on but for the wet.
Yes, the rains are again. The bed

is mounted by porchlight. So I can't sleep
says translucent eyelids, like awkward fish
where the ocean drained. To his I do

I do the bed like a sheet. That the cord can dictate light
we don't complain about. What long fingers
margin his touch,
dedicated as this bulb
to fishing

my waking. He sleeps through
and through, like a good kind
of genuine—that is not proof
the gold is

Big Fun

It's been a month since you came on my stomach and there
is starting to miss you. Soap goes on. Sweaters go on.
Bruises go on bourgeoning into brown flower-throats.
Elbow. Esophagus. Go on, abandon them. I like bars
that are named unsuspectingly, where you might find
yourself without meaning: Rickshaw Stop, Pete's Candy
Store, the Office, the Pharmacy Bar, the Library, Big
Fun. The ambulance bay is standing wide open, gurney
straps loose, syringes uncorked, each unstuck bandage
a tongue candy-white. Best friends are at the ready for
impulse, for injury. What will it do to her? The others
left marks. Here lover. Here line. I once had an end-stop.
The ultrasound, running over my thighs, rubbed hard
to see echo. On the screen: a tented city. On the screen:
a clotted vein. In the blood, in the body, I am hard little
stars. Beneath your gaze, I am naked and you understand.
With your head on my stomach, with my tongue in your
hair. Your heart is strong, but you were not there yet.
Salt was not there yet in stripes, in abandon. We were
clothed and in corners. We were making up minds.
For the minds, for the making, for the cloth-bundled
nerves, for the calcium deposits, for the clavicle which
burns, for the red, for the white, for the raw, for the stars,
for the Pharmacy and Rickshaw, for the danger
and the verve, for the verse and the finish, I would lie,
I would lie, I would lie down for you. Awwwwwww yeah.

Alison Pelegrin

Talk to the Hand

You don't have to sing in me, but bring it here,
spit it, spell it out, give up the goods,

poison the well with alphabet soup. Be good now,
and stab me in the back with bathroom talk,

stumble to your soapbox and throw me a bone.
I understand you when you speak in tongues—

open your clap trap and stutter with your shoes
unbuckled. Talk in your sleep. Toe it in the sand.

Blind me with little white lies. Bring a gavel
and bust up the filibuster in my brain.

It's time to kiss and make up. Give me a title
and I'll take it from the top. Hey you sassafras,

hey sweet thing—remember me? Before you say
so long, sayonara, toss me the dregs, drop a line

out of nowhere, lipstick in the mirror,
and let it tumble when I least expect it.

Pomegranate, Juiced

He tells me, *Squeeze it. Like this*, hands it to me,
cupping with my fingers, squeezing with my hand.

This squeezing into dew drinkable from the red cup
of itself, the leathery orb hand-like,

is like I'm squeezing his hand. I juice rubied knuckles
and tension's released. He hands me a knife

to *Pierce it. Right there*. With it I tease the skin, open
a little wound. *Put your mouth there – No. Give me your hand*.

He shows me how to make it flow. I draw it in.
Good?, he asks. I answer not simply

about the fruit, about its juice. About the wanting.
About wanting his hands to me.

Notes About His Hands

1.

Could I even tell how it was,

his hip on mine against the wall, my hands

shaking, had I ever touched him that

way in some other life, was his skin

always so hot to the touch, the shirt

I shoved my hands under;

Could I even touch him how he was,

shaking, my hand against the hot wall

of his hip, had I been

his shirt in some other life, was I always

so hot to the touch like something

he would shove against;

Could I tell him to make it even,

my hip shoved against the wall

of his hands, shaking, had I always

been so hot in another life to tell

how it was, to be the skin

under his touch;

Robyn Art

Could I even tell his hip from my hand,

shaking, had he ever

touched me in some

other life, was his shirt always a wall

against my hand, could he

shove me under

          *

            2.

Amorous: hot breath, the bra unfastened, skin like a nest of thorns,
scent of wood smoke, milk, a tussle of decomposing leaves

Savage: did not attend the termination

Redundant: the couch, the beer

Savage: this won't hurt a bit

Amorous: the bodies of women on trains

Redundant: don't ask me again

Savage: hot breath, the bra refastened, skin like a nest of thorns,
rain, the shape of water

Remorseful: the flowers, the beer

Remorseful: Yours, Truly &

Redundant: the leaves are back on the trees

       *

3.
(What to Do When You Can't Forget His Hands)

1) Order your steak bloody, your whiskey, straight up.

2) Purchase sensible things you've needed for some time: ink cartridge, rain gear, vacuum-cleaner bags.

3) Picture him tasting the congealed frosting of wedding cake samples, talking to the blonde-tipped florist, checking his watch every fifth word.

4) Remember all the places his hands have (haven't) been and all the places you wish his hands have (haven't) been.

5) Take long baths.

6) Make dinner for the man you live with. Manage (a record) not to burn the sauce.

7) See him everywhere: hotel bars; the laughter of people on trains; the dopey, blanked-out eyes of the Krispy Kreme guy.

8) Floss.

9) Take to drinking sherry in the tub while leafing through women's magazines. Learn to mulch, prevent rug burn, undo a zipper with your teeth.

10) Buy a rubber plant on sale. Manage (a record) to keep it alive for a month.

11) Recall, in the dark, the warmth of his mouth on your neck, the warmth of his neck on your mouth.

12)   Picture him, again, the only way you know how: standing
        around the portico, fumbling with the lighter, his
        shoulders hunched against the wind and beyond him the
        water, always the water…

                    *

                    4.
            (Elegy for his Hands)

It was late, I was drunk, you were warm

to my hand, I would say, please

don't leave, touch me there, but

you never

I was late, you were drunk, it was warm

to my hand, I would want, just

to please, you were there, but

I never

I was warm, you were late, it was drunk

to my touch, I was just

late to want, but I would

leave you never

                    *

Gary L. McDowell

Gymnosperm

A girl molds him of wetted clay,
his arms in direct proportion
to his legs. She carves her initials
into his brow then makes lean his torso,
his pelvis full and exact, wide, too full,
until his limbs start to fold in on themselves
like a dying sunflower. She deepens
and deepens the eyes on his forehead–
her fingers are cold, his tongue is dirty–
if she were to scrape it down,
would her fingerprints melt into that stratum
and become his taste. She gives
an extra kiss of flesh and lips
depress, the ridges in each rut enough
to tighten his spine. His neck clicks.
The ball of one bone kneads the other.
But her hands ache for something to hold.
The body is now planted.

Molly Tenenbaum

My Tender Heart

To dough, take
a biscuit cutter:
lift the lid. It's gooey
jelly under.

Pot pie, jam tart,
hot bun's inner butter.
Its evidence is
that I think in syrup and batter.

It's shapeless, abashed,
a dribbled bib.
Loose as the tongue's
unmouthed blob.

From here you can't see
the whole watershed,
or if underground
magma boils blue or red,

or the violin,
though arpeggios weep
from an afterschool house
down the street.

Pends from a stem
in snowdrop fragility:
starry eyes, forget-me-not,
the checkered lily,

and like the starred windshield
of my car, old, that must keep running.
"Sure," says my genius
mechanic, pointing

to his own in the dark
through the shop door,
far older than mine,
and he's kept it roaring

four hundred thousand miles and counting.

Ashley VanDoorn

Vamp

It is always arrival at the castle after
treefuls of bats echo-spell a hex trestleworked into our tundra beds.
"I am nothing if not pleasing,"
said this coal-steeped beast, snowy neckskin slipping up my may I cut in
to the frozen go-stab-yourself dance,
interject the bones she poses in her hair playfully but not carefree?

The shape of my bluff my shroud—
gruff little eyeteeth, grieving-tough she fucks not as lasting cure nor
last clear lyric, not lake metric
nor lash curve. She flattens me as I hone my flattery to care
not for topknots but yes for coattails
and wax the past is ever slick like a series of slips unslipperied serious.

Several-faced we know to wear
fumbling bloodshot, otherwise known as *spilling blooms a dark*
redemption we dye brighter our cares
away she is a porno and pavements are a mess. I may be impressed with
her pierced-erotics as our virgins
desert, but I sleep tight—*grim ride for grand times*. Pale contrast safely
delays cape-dipped with lip-drippier.
Barely-touchables command astray a distance too in charge
          to interchange
the sickly excited music we sip sick.

She's all a bit spinning like any dulling fastness, thus our
          disciplined rage
for boredom poured into a black broth
she ladles into our nightmare mouths in the months of
          nightly unhousing.
I wander chamber to even secreter
passage and waste wine on my tongue my bliss my what long
belief you have. Two tines valued at who

can define sublime sucked and sucked us dry is so desire. Three
       bites become

you breaking away to stay the feeder I like
her fading wrinkles and lack of bareness best but the rest is sexy, and
       makes a kind
of recognition to me. Why can't she be
from the sea? Craving is merely fire over water, or mind sweating
       over time,
time which diced me a gamble double-crossed
by a defender for live-forever. How to want to die when Satisfy
       says otherwise?

Supposing the lonely last-supper together
in her ice-jungle, it would be okay to meet briefly love brimming over
       the melting
canopy, which is only a frosted lawn,
and we are shrunk together we have drunk too much unto
       needing machines
to bleed life spent with fencemates.
We think speaking, our guilt exotic as first clockwork wakes vanes into
       vines I vale
as the lost game-piece. Please
de-bone me. Less solid I could devour her awaiting feastial sacrifice.

She'S turning me around She SliverS into my Shimmering bedclotheS
She breakS my Silver watch StopS my pretenSe of time She circleS
inSide teacheS me to drive my miStreSS She miS-StreSSed She
StreSSed my trying to fight Such delight in the way She biteS with her
entire mouth the Scavenger of our union iS a temptreSS She wantS
without Searching my more labyrinthine

blood is and is not bond—I beg you—bail me out
into what you spy I spy—in slowhand—speech I wish to send you
before I know if I like it, but I wish too much. Too many
I's lead to suicide, some study said—I say she likes without loving,

Ashley VanDoorn

which *is* pleasure,
and all this written on her
pleases and deepens a wound we've groomed to channel her
     cry me a groove
from departure point
to pressure part—I plea to see—after she left for the first few days we
     were babble
and then the babble began
to (de)mean us, asking what every wannabe wonders: what does it feel
     like when people
fall asleep to your face?

Jennifer L. Knox

If My Love for You Were an Animal

It would have three legs left, but only need two.

It would be easy to catch, but hard to kill.

It could hold its breath all winter and sleep upside down, anchored under the ice in kelp.

When wet, it would smell like clarinet reeds.

It would break every thing in the house—but purposely, silently, secretly, one item at a time, over hundreds of years, so no one would notice.

Its cry, like an electrical tower wrestling a giant tinfoil dolphin in a meteor crater; its purr, low enough to drive snakes from their dens.

It would be flightless, but you could always find it hiding up high.

Its name would mean magnet. Ants would march towards it over mountains, and across the sea floor.

You could elbow it as hard as you wanted to right in the ribs.

It would be so loyal, if you fell asleep before you took the sleeping pill, it would slip the sleeping pill under your tongue.

Erika Meitner

Treatise on Dwelling

There must be a place where everyone
is slippery and lovely and not
up all night. There must be a place
that's less work than this,
where something compels you
other than comfort and highways
with just two lanes which
won't snap back or fold
in on themselves like a fitted sheet,
lumped and faded, warm from the dryer.
Everything in the laundromat
is hot in summer—your head
inside the machine for a moment
to reach the one sock trapped
in back, ear-drum echo.
(Like the echo of your voice
might take you back into the right
dark cave if only you could breathe
more quietly?) The echo started
on a bench by the bay, when he
arranged his head in your lap.
In the photo, you look worried, not brave.
A brave transistor radio balanced on his chest.
Your fingers rested on his face.
The face of the radio played static.
The static radio played big band.
The band-radio channeled the sound
of cable cars, the shiver of metal wires,
mechanical ocean anticipation, waves
of Rube Goldberg or Golgi apparatus—
the apparatus of every bad motel from here
to the next place called home. Home

is the one who spends more time
trying to find you than anyone else.
Rest there. Choose him.

Sunlight or Sunshining

The whole follows the half
The half follows the invisible to no end

The torn photo creates double a world

Is it "don't know what I am doing" again?
What I am is a big bag of skin flesh

I go out into the yard
I go out into the street

In the sunlight out by the yard, by the stream
warming my eyes, the sunlight can control everything,
at once and not at all

And waiting
Waiting

You are just laughing on the corner in your mind thinking
of all the people you used to know, then emptying

The voices and the winding up
Those faces that fade

The sunshine hopes for the last sighting
of opera sky and distraction

The last laugh is it?
It is not there

Lift your skinny arms to me, soft
in overhanging leaves, moths

Erik Sweet

Under the eaves I hear a sun cough

The only bridge and I cherish the actual light
The sun and my skin, heating up and then eventually
going back inside me for warmth

My eyeing light words on a moment that
is still

May 2005

Katie Fesuk

Why We Missed the Lunar Eclipse

England 1999

An ocean away, Abby's blood still sinks
into a windowpane of the oldest building in Oxford,
pools like congealed soup—that drop of her
(or who she thought she was) the night she drank sherry
at Jesus' College Pub and wondered
if she would feel any less crazy
with her hand on the other side of a window.

She rocked on a dorm chair,
surrounded by dog-eared Brönte and Woolf.
We wrapped her wrist in toilet paper
while she moaned, Stop the madness, somebody
stop the goddamned madness,
wine stains darkening the corners of her mouth.
She may as well have asked for the Queen.

In a room where emergencies happened,
we slept through dawn's lunar eclipse
while Abby's flesh was stitched together.
Others asked about the bandage, the blood trail
on cobblestone leading to her room. We said,
oh, it was a game, an accident... and hid
her cries like Catherine's on the moor.

At her wedding years later, I wondered
if her husband would ever know
that a drop of his wife's blood
seeps and sinks deeper into oak
just meters away from the Bodleian,
wondered if he knew about that pane across the ocean,
if he could be jealous of wood.

Mark DuCharme

Poem

To be remiss I have to shake you up
Until profligate women impact summer
In the din of summer will you go away
I think so intimately polyvocal in height
What are colors? Are they embedded in light?
What limits poem's semblance to the blonde
Provoked in sleight of radiance to its gaze
Who are also unattractive, though we skid
& The nearly full moon is upside down
Eclipsed by what, remembered, we undid

Mary Biddinger

Copper Harbor

Freakish, like a tapestry.
The dark smudge of fish
shanties and smokehouses.
An orange nylon jacket

knotted on the breakwater.
We saw the people, made
change for their twenties.

The seagulls were quick
as equinox, Evinrude,
flypaper lit with a zippo.

All cabins have the same
linoleum. It's universal.
I took prints with knees
and palms. Read your tale

of botanical swerve, flash
and fragment. Artichoke
or parsnip? The ether surge

of a mower on the parkway
slapped us out of reverie.
I asked you the sound

of fishhook through a lip.
You gave me a silver cup
and claw hammer. I woke

all night inspecting corners,
nasturtiums. Your body
an arrow into the lake.

Jenny Browne

In Some Pregnant Dreams

You must leave Africa today
or maybe it's China, wherever
you carry a leaky burlap sack of eels
then watch them writhe fire-like
in the bus's crowded aisle.
No shit. No suitcase. No sushi.
No warning when you're let off
at the familiar high school to find
a standby ticket home. You forge
the signature fine but there's a long
line outside the attendance office.
Listen up people, I don't have all day.
But you have all night. Deep in
the humid gymnasium, the dance team
can't get their high kicks in line
and your first boyfriend crouches
under the bleachers nursing
a spotty beard. He looks up
and says you were a good lay.
You weren't. But you were seventeen.
You were good for anything, even lying
in the scratchy grass near the triple-jump-pit.
It's still field day and you win a three
-legged race alone. Somewhere in the distance
your name crawls itself through the megaphone
and the drum major who is your mother who
is your grandmother who is wearing
a sky-blue wool hat explains that the sneezes,
second spine, webbed feet and bag of elbows
doe-see-doeing inside you, honey,
that's real.

Michelle Detorie

Honey Suck Carousel

O, Honey Suck
the air is bare
and clean as a pole
from which the horse
rides. The horse moves

up and down until
the wheel returns.
Twirl of my hair
in your mouth.
You tasting the dirt.

We were the wheel.
The world on its teeter—
our tongue-junks
marking the milk
of the swell with an "X."

A bind spun from floss
of the bridle. The mare's
eyes moored in their sockets,
the swill of the swirl. Your
eyes unbuttoned my

sweater, unfastened my
locket. Foal of forgetting
ungalloped at our side. I pulled
the reins, you tore the veil.
The world whizzed by, in lace.

Allyson Salazar

Pink Taco

From my perch on the silk wood dock
I watch your preparations—

towel, water, then keys
and shoes buried in a bush,

before slipping into
the body of your
cunt-shaped kayak.

Paddle tips tear the young water
stroking your way forward.

I don't know your history
but it's clear you're experienced;

as if this kayak vagina
might have birthed you

bobbing on the surface
smiling wide and open
turned into the wind.

If I slap your ass as you glide past
it's to confirm your perfect entrance at a far shore.

Morgan Lucas Schuldt

My More Merely

In this surround, above the downs,
are my kind of live.

An *mmhmm* her
fever-few-&-far-between.

Cherry get, if gotten you be.
Otherhow unhindered by the things

of me. Things like: junk-hold lungs,
bouts with *be*, the *umm*-hush & long static of kinda can.

Are twenty-six flavors of *-elicious*
& what-if's head-fuck nagging blood-back for more

cream & rush, heave & shush––
dirt-back glares having some pull over the percentages.

No tut-tut strut, no lapse in gush. Just holier than wow––
an old-fashioned dumb-lovely *ah yes!* suitable for basking.

Sheer towardness, my raredear, I'd sky-write
a surrender for.

Little red likelihooded
I lust so much.

the gogo dancer speaks

I. how legs work

my body a slick
tool and Vaseline
on my teeth so I smile
I stand just behind
the stage before
the song begins
legs in fishnets
tight as tiny ropes
and a feeling
like a fall
on ice when a body
does the inevitable-
the follow through
of what's already
in motion

II. how eyes work

watching
you watch me
to a hammer
everything's a nail
my eyes aren't mirrors
of my soul
mirrors are where
you look to see yourself
I know what you are
looking for in my eyes
and I won't ask you later
what color they are
everyone wants to be nailed
when they're hammered

Malaika King Albrecht

III. how a mouth works

kissing a stranger
is like biting
aluminum foil
with metal fillings
sharp tingles
I know I shouldn't
enjoy
before I kiss him
the moment
before tasting too
tart lemonade
I know I'll drink
because my mouth's
already decided

Shann Palmer

At the Museum, Molly

reads poems long and thin
as her loblolly legs
rise from the hardwood floor.

With a mouth full of feathers,
she hums Dulce Domum,
the air tastes like fresh pears.

I would embrace her there
while the sun slides into the wall,
touch behind her ear, treasure her

until a draught takes the words
off the page onto our skin.
Then we will feast on syllables

in front of a new acquisition;
the statue of a faceless woman,
Jaipur marble perfectly carved.

Jenna Cardinale

Is a Rose

My forehead ages
into a staircase.

I am armed
against artificial
roses.

But there is an ouch
in this inoculation.

Reach down to my vanilla.
Be sweet and traditional.

Crush 19

the cinema is cruel / like a miracle
Frank O'Hara

Her smirk & catch what dangle before
cigarette, his con's eye & lips working
toothpick, the locked door, the absent
husband, loaves & dough still perfect
or rising, his face implied in her thighs'
diamond, palm's thrust, knife flung, C'mon—
helping him help himself to shank
of neck, kneading breasts, the garter,
her stockings, his grip & squeeze between,
a tight shot the camera wont' release
(us) until we, we—wonder: is this love
for Cora Papadaukis & Frank
Chambers where the heart is crushed living
vagabond & bound, resuscitated
in lust, when at a roadside station,
they wait for neon, drink coffee,
how she says do I look Greek to you?

Julie R. Enszer

Imagining the Nipples of the Famous Male Poet

They are small. Surrounded, now, by all gray hair.
They are pink. Stark points on his otherwise translucent skin.
They are flaccid. Usually; though he always thinks of them erect.
They are tough. Not soft and tender like the plums of his youth.
They are wrinkled. Skin sagging slightly over his atrophied chest.
They are covered. Beneath the corduroy blazer he donned for
        this workshop.
They are not like my father's. Although he fancies my
        Electra complex.
They are not like my wife's. Hers are mine. His, not yet.

Bruce Covey

Spell Your Name

I draw your name on the blackboard 50 times
I see it in the rapid flapping of blackbird wings
I script it in the setting concrete between bricks
I spend it within the confines of this knick knack shop

Get lots of items for it & inscribe your name on each
Put them on shelves with your labels underneath
Drag myself through the swampy torrent of your name
Landscape caused by your consonants and vowels
The phonemes someone new to this map might utter

Yet stranger still, sensing some kind of center
Lack of ambiguity somewhere, addressed
Somehow through paperwork fingerprints credit
History photographs blood type net contribution

Steve Mueske

Tangerines

He holds the weight of the fruit
           in his palm, gently peels off
the thin skin and slides his thumb

inside. Slowly he presses the sodden slice
           into her mouth,
past the warm lips, the slightest brush

of teeth. He watches her eyes close
in that brief drift of pleasure
           that is taste,
           that is wanting by another name, time

slowed to its essence. And then her jaws
           are working, a concert
of 117 muscles and skin, movement of birdlike

bones and subtle shifts of light. He feeds her
another
           and another, quicker now,
                  and she laughs
and wipes the dribble from her chin, slaps

away his hand. Outside, the birds flit
           from branch to bush, carrying on
a conversation that has no beginning or end. It is,

after all, like the room we return to, filled
with a strangely private
           language. See how the light spins

           with dust over the torn rind
piled like discarded clothes on the plate.

How Eve Was Created

you pour water over the small Asian fern, *Cheilanthes argentea*, to see if it will cry out in pain. you deliver electric shocks to the sidecar below actual dance fragment mnemonic and calcite splinter: the trolley-pull sweat locker of greenhouse

you learn that daylight is a card game of raindrops. you poke at the caterpillar because you read somewhere that it would turn into a firefly and play "lost little" choruses all afternoon, until the air goes completely out of its color

you break cigarettes over an open gas flame to witness cancer belonging to its owner, "chipped" as they say, or "inseminated." the moon is a prostate valve most stubborn at its recital, argument sliding scale performance review at its apogee— eyes as hearsay, trivial things we must put up with

you hitch your heart to a wagon and tell the driver only to stop once on the way. Charleston, South Carolina. and when he does, it is at a reconstructed plantation where frogs lie on their backs on the burning plot of lawn (think vegetable garden at midnight)

you imagine that an alternative to witchcraft would be silence. that's it. just silence. and after the smell from ballet rooms wafts out on Lysol towels, you find an herb that Marie Selby herself couldn't bear the aroma of

you check on the fern, see how it's doing. buy it a get-well card the size of a building. it won't thank you. she will sit there with her arms crossed and demand another pitcher of ice water. and you'll say go find yourself another private room, this one is taken. for this is the afternoon I plan to have my rib removed

Peg Duthie

Coat

If he took off his glasses, it would be more
than a layer removed between his eyes and mine,
more than the blend of myopia and lust
blurring the curbs we continue to erect —
do not cross. do not enter.
do not touch. no food or drink allowed.

It would be just enough to become too much
so I prefer the devastation of his polished
remove, his eyes acknowledging all we haven't said
as he smoothly drapes his jacket over my shoulders
even though I haven't let him see me shiver.

Didi Menendez

When I Said Goodbye

I was making arroz con pollo.
I was making espumita for my café.
I was stirring the pot while the gizzards
and neck wrapped in cellophane
waited to become crisp in hot olive oil.

I was grinding garlic into the oregano with a mortar.
I was sipping Robert Mondavi chardonnay.

My daughter sucked the juice out of all the limes.

I drove to Publix for new limes.
They were on special four for a dollar.
I contemplated Double Stuff Oreo cookies.
I waited for the check out girl to break my twenty.
The grocery bagger said hello to my children.
The grocery bagger asked if I needed help.
I wanted to say yes.
I need help.

I used the change to fill my Cherokee.
When I said goodbye,

There was a bald man sending me poetry.
There was a monk in Tibet dancing to poetry.
There was a lonely woman in San Francisco
jumping off the Golden Gate Bridge.

When I made it back to the arroz con pollo,
I rejected the bald man's poetry.
I was not empathetic.
I turned off the music.
I turned on the stove.

Didi Menendez

I fed the turtles.
I gave some nibbles to the dogs.
I threw a bone to the cat.
I looked outside my kitchen window.
The mango tree is still barren.

You with your full head of hair.
You with your perfect smile.

Me left to suck on a chicken neck alone.

Andrea Potos

I Return to You

I leave him and come home
to the mound of your clothes in the basket,
clean and left from Saturday's laundry.
In our pale blue room, a sprawl of ivory
roses on our bed, I spread them all
around me—the cotton T-shirts and socks
you wear to the gym each morning, your jeans
with the hole in the back pocket where your wallet pokes out.
I press your shirts to my face, their worn nap
easy on my skin. I fold them and match them
shoulder to shoulder, pat them down in our
cedar drawer—the burnt orange and smoke blue,
olive green that reflects the gold in your hair
like tiger's eye.
I breathe in the clean rinse of you
like a deep and necessary sleep where I know
I could never live this quiet with him, never smooth out his socks
roll them up, like firm white buds
he could unfurl every morning.

Parlor

The undertaker is young, attractive—
your type. Sharp suit. Muted tie.

The kind of moment where I'd imagine
you'd make a joke about things that are "stiff,"

meaning you, except it's true:
you've made it onto your back for him
and it's golden, those moments of you

stripped in the backroom where it's always
a little too cool.

The undertaker asks, "Would you like to view the body?"
But I've seen you.

The air around the body is cold. You chill it.
My neck is cold. The blank coins of your eyes
have been removed.

He's laced your fingers
incorrectly. You're left-handed:
left thumb goes on top. A lover would know
these little details, like how

this isn't the first time
you've worn lipstick.

Your hair remains immaculate.
You mannequin, you. In your new black suit.

You, mannequin, on your back.
No one's going to love you like this—

Function of Senses

Redlight Lamplight

Pretend I'm the one that brung you
here and kick all else like a danger.
In the natural world, colors slip
off to "disremember," grow
poisonous in the backs
of cars. The place I'm from dangles
in a home-made mosquito
light, and every girl camps
evenings in her own wet halo.
In the natural world, suits slouch
off themselves, children go to
the Jungle Room to skunk
the way of dreams.
When we get too far gone
I am going to swing you.
You are going to let me.

Phil Crippen

The Tattoo I Didn't Get

trapped in a blizzard
of   mink-clad
nymphs
drowsy with donor
fatigue
in the land of
edward
scissorhands
where   the
infomercial is king
as instinctive as a
vine
in the blue marble
organism
which doesn't allow
the other—
the sea or the shore?
"this is me," says
she,
saying 'good-bye'
and   the   door
becomes murky
and I've seen this
murk before
is anyone asking
questions
anymore?
while   in
this   détente
you give me a
"pre-emptive strike"
so how are we
supposed to be

a six-legged couple?
right now, I'm going
to   go
into town and rape
some
grand pianos
intention   is   one
thing
effect is another
but nobody's name
goes   on
the small of my
back!

Deborah Ager

Nothing

Nothing will make me screw you one more time.
Not a rose, a note, your hands or president.
Who knew that loving you was worth a dime?

You make my favorite soup; you serve me wine
And blackness saunters in; my words are spent.
Nothing will make me screw you one more time.

I could wander in your garden, gnaw on thyme
Yet still I'd think in love you're, well, dormant.
Who knew that loving you was worth a dime?

I dreamed you pushed me and I couldn't climb
Up from bed. You said it wasn't what you meant.
Nothing will make me screw you one more time.

Now I'm sucking down a drink infused with lime.
—To think I dreamed of cakes encased in fondant.
Who knew that loving you was worth a dime?

How glad I am never to have returned to you one time,
Because already your name, on my tongue, is absent.
Nothing will make me screw you one more time.
Who knew that loving you was worth a dime?

that roses bud wild in me

and I drunken
amnesia devoured
by the tiniest petal
silence searing open eyes
and vertigo where
I call you
my obliteration
my speech
woman of disappearances
to speak of mutual dedications
delicate, trespass of garden
evasion, night's heart
reciprocal
tenderness and
trembling
ignorant as speech
still
distilled

Ana Bozicevic-Bowling

Document

The roses are so still. Their nightly heads navigate
a tub of unease, star-tall.

Who stamped the passports of these hordes of spring?
The traveler's oarless, crests on a promise.

The blue chart rolls off the cabin table.
(Shhh.) Ship sheds boats. The roses were too much.

He can always find work as a statue, or moonlight
as museum night-guard. Through greenery, days,

he still walks the park, in a scarf,
unaware he was made to endure…

And look: roses wait, the widowers.
Their brief terms are Nordic, a violin concerto.

Each is a number: an ardor in order.
Like them he is measured against pearly histories.

Releases that rudder. A little bit lower—
(You've almost forgotten—): There, we've both signed it.

He plays at being a thorn.

Bread

1.
Of course you'd have money
for a suite with French furniture
fake but not embarrassing,
the lily prints framed against walls
bland but not offensive,
the King-sized bed encased in gold cloth
but not repelling like *sateen*,
a foyer tiny but marbled with interesting veins,
an ice bucket with a monograph—
this is as good as it gets
for hotel rooms meant for an afternoon tryst

You're the one who knows better
than to cuddle afterwards

Five minutes afterwards,
your face is as bland as the wallpaper
to hide your impatience as, your pale palm
chilling my bare elbow,
you guide me to the door.
I marveled at your courteous mask
so much I forgot
you are not
the poet on a deadline
I almost missed for three
twenty-dollar-bills.

Eileen R. Tabios

2.
I would have refunded your
tax-free money
if you'd cuddled afterwards
because of larger things at stake
when birthing a poem.

In this alternative scenario
this poem would have been about lilies—
how some look like neophyte nuns,
how others mimic the carved folds
ending the skirts of Virgin Marys,
how Georgia O'Keefe never succeeded
in painting them as abstract vaginas
(vaginas can never be abstract),
how their scent evokes the type of decay
lurking in candle-soaked shrines
measuring the dusk permeating marble churches

how the red pistil rising
from waxy white petals
always look profane
and magnificently divine.

Alison Pelegrin

Breaking Curfew with the Ancient Chinese Poet

drunk we lie down in empty hills,
heaven and earth our quilt and pillow
Li Po

If it weren't for poetry you'd be so lame
against my knack for braiding cherry stems
with my tongue. You want me on your team so bad
you're pitching stones like Romeo below my window—
won't I be your sidekick since I have a fake I.D.?
Just like a high school boy, the way you ask me out
then make like I'm invisible, shooting pool,
waiting for daiquiri number two to kick in.
And what good is a joker without his mate,
a sixteen year old fool enough to shimmy down
the trellis and flatfoot through the thorny bushes,
yes her only language. Yes, the moon's an eyelash.
Yes, Bourbon Street, and the strippers tease
at first because I'm a foot taller and we're both
wearing Chinaman pajamas. Relax, teacher,
and learn by watching how to swap with tourists—
kisses for Southern Comfort. We pass tallboys
and cigarettes around a circle of unnamed friends
and I'm beyond caring that it's four a.m.
We should keep on, tallying flinches
from the silver mime over coffee and beignets.
Anything but home. One whiff of me
and it'll be lockdown in the guest bedroom
with nothing for fun but childhood games,
all of them missing pieces. Two weeks
of Battleship, Yatzee, and the doodles
in my notebook—Lady Po. A. Po. A. P.

Clay Matthews

Pablo Neruda I Saw You in a Picture Once

Blossom and spring sprung,
I want you, in silence, to do,

to do: (I want, what I want,
I want) to do to you

what the cinema does
to the darkness, to the much less,

to the revival of the image
of the unlit, the unlived

the unthere (under there). (What I want,
I want) which is to say

(to do) I will hold you
(to do) the way the curtain

(I want) holds the call.

Michael Farrell

the hallelujans

she & he couldnt
love theyd tried it before
not with each other though
no, other women other men.

they could just as well,
drown-sadly, as pray for love.
he was cold which had its
satisfactions she was in fragments, like newspaper.

– a dove, or a book
lit their skins up
skins or minds or
grasped their soft shoulders, – stopped their cruising.

– they pulled their stomachs in.
she let down her guard &
he began to look at others,
& praise & not rate.

whenever the rain lifted theyd be
out there: <<making-small talk!>>
– & getting so uncomfortable
the spirit must arrive soon!

– ive been there you too,
in the showers of love:
– just one word is all
it takes: <<hello! im naked its refreshing! ...

Michael Farrell

<<naked, i have to go & study but ...>>
— the risks are extreme ill admit that
but once you, think you can make
anything work still hang on for smitten ...

— theres a word for
all of us seeking flirting
selfconceived hallelujans practising our virtues
mostly, ladies gentlemen, never mean.

Christine Scanlon

That Hiccup was Optimism

there might have been other dimensions to know

rather than this one world walking around
with her long face—

    showing all the joy of a love-object
embedded in half closed eyes.

It seems we were both tired of being
moved—

    of wearing holes on the outside
of our dress—someone else
always pulling the strings

intermittently—but Ouch!

Aaron Belz

The Glass Slipper and the Fly

"I don't want to be transparent,"
said the glass slipper to the fly.

"Honest, maybe. Not see-through."
And the fly in a tiny voice replied,

"Which fairy tale is it, exactly,
in which a glass slipper talks to a fly?"

"Look," said the slipper, "I like you,
okay? Stop fucking around.

I just don't want you to think
that you can sleep with me

just because I'm obvious about how I feel
or that there's not more to me

than meets the eye. There's a lot
you don't know, little fly."

And the fly stilled his wings
and seemed to ponder these things.

"I don't want to be transparent
either," he said, looking away.

"I'm embarrassed to talk about it.
I don't want to appear weak.

But listen, I like you a lot too.
I'm not trying to get you in the sack."

Aaron Belz

The slipper was wise to the ways
of the fly, who, like all other flies,

knew the right thing to say.
But she liked him anyway.

Michael Meyerhofer

Shame as Proof of True Love

For J.

A lonely man could watch
a beautiful woman wipe her own ass,
then make love to her afterwards
and feel good about himself,
but real love, I've decided, is when
you see your lover at their most
awkward, wretched moments
and still want to fuck them later.

The gulf between making love
and fucking need not be explained
here, of course, since anyone
reading poetry has already been
shell-shocked into this market,
but tell Freud I said it's better to be
a wise ape than a horny seraph.
Love, I am addicted to you

the way some crave heroin
even before they taste its saccharin
kiss, and I know we're in love
because I want to fuck you to cinders,
to lap dry all that's holy in you,
then, even after my shameful crash,
I wake with my face held
between your cappuccino thighs.

Josh Hanson

At the Movies

They taught the pigs to handle money:
to lift with feeling lips a coin and place
it into bank or box—the action is all—
and the food to come after. The pigs
proved quick to learn, and capable perhaps
of metaphor, they soon forgot their task:
they would only root the coins hungrily,
so sweetly it now reeked of food:
and the blank-faced boy behind the counter
sells me trash at outrageous cost:
concessions, they're called, in memory of a time
before all fell under one wide reach,
before we came always to feed like this:
our mouths full of silver, noses to the ground.

Timothy Bradford

My Secret Fantasy Life

Cheryl, the dental assistant,
welcomes me, is
real nice, makes me feel
right at home. She wears
scrubs, latex gloves, a blue paper mask
and clear plastic eye protection.
She asks about
problem areas, and when she
has me down, my
mouth open wide and a large
dental pick scraping the grooves
on some sensitive tooth
in the back, she asks if I've
been to the State Fair yet.

I nearly gag answering
with my tongue trying to lie down,
be polite, not follow her work
all over my mouth like a needy
dog. So I take to grunting. She
seems to like it, responds by
asking more questions, increasing
the pressure and speed
of the dental pick until it begins
to nick at my gums here
and there. Behind
the too-big mirrored sunglasses
she's given me for protection,
I close my eyes and remember
that scene in *The Marathon Man*.
Cheryl could ruin my mouth
with a quick slip.
My leg twitches. I sweat.

And imagine Cheryl, about
the same age as my wife,
astride me. She wears
her turquoise dental assistant's top,
nothing else, and rocks gently
back and forth, like a chambered
nautilus swims, as she works.
Fear and eroticism are fine bed mates.
She stops asking questions, works
with an intensity that feeds
my fantasy, almost makes the minute,
enormous pain bearable.

I want to open my eyes
and look at her, but when I do,
my fantasy goes askew. She's
at the wrong angle, has the wrong
grimace on her face, looks
like she could be scrubbing
the neck of some little kid in a tub,
determined beyond the kid or dirt or
tooth or husband or job that involves
looking into hundreds of mouths, all
with their own unique
mouth smell, weekly. So I
close my eyes again, try to
imagine the pressure of her body
over me. She is slender but fairly
tall and would weigh more
than you would think.

My fear? Vagina dentata? No, not teeth there. The teeth in our very
own mouths. The labiodental and linguadental sounds—*this fit,
that fête, this fat, that fought, this foot*—and their absence. The way
we're born to gum, then chew, then, if we're lucky? gum again. The

singularly oracular symbolism of the mouth and the phantasms of
worlds it spews. Teeth in a kiss, or more so, a kiss without teeth.
These little enamel plates of *clack-clack* that fall out, hide under
pillows, mutate into coins, scintillate in the sun, work against the
tongue, with the tongue, "by these teeth I thee wed," the stain, the
decay, the loss. A weak spot in some god's plan, like knees. Or is it
just our sin of sugar? *Oh, little white sweets of sin, please stay firm in
the sulci.*

Cheryl finishes. I am awake and sitting
upright, talking to the dentist.
She says, Everything looks great, and I agree.
The sun, breaking through the clouds,
reveals a single bullet mark
in the glass before us, but the surface
still has integrity, keeps
the animals out
though they can see,
relaxed, grimacing, done,
us through the glass, window
to our interior human world.

Cosmopolitan Poet

At dinner somebody laid the phrase "pubescent bubble"
across the table, and the surge of it knocked out my lights.
Now, in the dark, I paint landscapes in Prussian blue
and my brushes are doctored Q-tips.
I wonder how Penelope managed all those years
alone in Ithaca. I can hear my aunt snore
like a goat in the next room, and I'm tired even thinking
about next Saturday's tea party and baby shower.
How did I get taken in by all this? I feel like I'm already late.

Kate Greenstreet

Book of Love

*"—then it turned into a flower, I don't understand.
It was a diamond outside."*

Leave openings

for entrance from the street.
"That's why they have conductors"

(those big tubes running underneath the floor).

In art, like sex, the unbidden
and the willingness.

(the melting point the boiling point the melting point)

They call to one another.
Maybe communicate with flashlights.

("Nobody else can make one like me. And now I'm gone.")

:

Eros is tired.
Was a god,
is a moon.

"Arlene came home with fifteen hundred dollars worth of gloves
and that was just one episode."

:

Crossed out:
Events here on earth.
I woke up.
are   so   I

We got wings.
Could somebody turn that down?

:

My vacation (reminiscing): Took a bath in brown water, cried for an hour. Sat on the linoleum, read some poems aloud. In a place where the windows stay open, my door is completely made of glass.

:

So much we say to one another isn't true—it's just the way it comes out, so we need to be forgiving.

My father was alive and was becoming a draftsman. He still had something to say about building. He'd lost something. That was important.

We'll carry it forward, he said, but separately. That same day we were teaching ourselves how to think about life. There was a trick to it.

:

"It's more like windows—or pictures, in a row."
Recurring dream of a numbered list.

400: Introverts

(to be alone, to be with their animals, to think about science)

:

"She's writing all the time, and she's carrying a suitcase.
She might be going somewhere." (my temporary
girlfriend: strong stress, weak pitch)

Kate Greenstreet

I couldn't find the empty diamond.
Remembering together provokes doubt.

"for pitch is like light
and colour

stress
like weight"

Scatters
the visible.

The diamond ring effect is seen just as totality
starts
and ends.

:

The person in the room who never speaks, I was
(appearing,
disappearing islands).
I understand in 5 languages.
I understand you, try a little harder.

"It's the 2 kinds of yellow."
"He's pissin' pollen."
"Some people have pretty patios."
"Don't believe so *much* in the ground, believe in the bone."

Ideas: That someone could know you, without
doing the work. That you can have a second chance
at life. What people say: "saved for a reason."
(He thought I meant the lettuce.)

I was back in the old kitchen, we were putting the dishes
away. We didn't seem
particularly close.

"You might have to learn how to lie without leaving the body.
Put *that* in your book of love."

:

Ice, it gets under your feet.
You don't know it's there.
I was thinking of Keats, Baudelaire.
I was thinking of boys.

Why are we ashamed when someone hurts us?
Because it marks us, as valueless.

I can't hear you man
you're breaking up
I'm losing you

who goes above
so this is all up or down wander wander

to find love
to "find" love
to find "love"

no eye   (sewn shut)
pig iron   (saw not)

Can it be true that a lump of coal, under tremendous
pressure, will become
a diamond?
That a block of ice, as it melts, moves forward?

Kate Greenstreet

It was my father
who put the reindeer up on the mirror, at Christmastime.
Think of him

in the way he'd *want* you to think of him
(as every treasure
wants to be hidden first, then found—
the same with every crime, they say)

:

The 3 Cs ("like the 7 Seas")
Clarity
Contact
Commitment—
you can do it!
with grammar,
code,
the kind of stuff that washes up,
trash,
the kind you'd never throw away, you'd never have it
in the first place.
Blue plastic bottles, two, like
from another country.
From another time.

:

One, the creative.
Nine in the second place.
"In the third place, I'm seven."
sand / pretend
The papers and the piece of
green material—
I got them, I got out of there.

two
the receptive

water

"rock
and language"

progress

what conducts
what carries

red

our hearts
our diamonds

black as pitch

:

I dreamed I lived in a very windy place. The trash just blew across
the kitchen floor, and there was nothing I could do about it. It was
such a windy place.

In the Mouth

Generosity and

pugilism have not

one thing in common, save

a soft "g." They manage

to find their way into

the same sentence, strange

bedfellows, as goes the

adage by some wayward

sage who yearned to believe

we are all connected.

Charity's stooge versus

organized rage. Gentle

consonant, why do you

insist on these cages?

Kim Young

You Smell Shalimar on His Neck Tie

The books say that in a good marriage the kids don't know.
A father works nights and has a laugh you can't forget: he whispers
and winks
when he comes home late, you can smell Shalimar on his neck tie.

The female body must be the situation, it must be the instrument.
Now that you are married, you understand this. Your dad gets
drunk and jokes
about his girlfriends. You see him winking at your husband.
In the end, your position is outside.

A mother smiles even when a father's back is turned. She pulls off
his belt
and throws his dirty jeans into the washer. She is like an empty
church. You go there for the cool pews and the lights
inside glass candles.

You are beautiful like the Russian girl in the magazine. She is
looking out from
inside her soldier's arms. She is calm and can hold the end
of a cigarette quietly in her fingers.

She is waiting for dark on the border of needing help
and needing nothing. You place the magazine back on the
nightstand,
shake out the laundry,
take your fingers to the ashes
that are falling.

Jenna Cardinale

The House

He places a bet on sunset,
on the highlights
in the brunette's hair.

He could not forget
his own body next
to hers. Wet with her sweat.

But this is roulette—
He readies himself
for regret, the threat
of a black or red upset.

Yet.

None of the doors I want
to enter open.

Olive eyes, red flecked,
ogle in their jars,
hug the pantry blush of
always summer.

He starts packing
in anticipation.

The water heater grumbles
in its dusty cupboard and
the cat won't even brush
her thrumming ribs against it.

He just starts stripping
the faux-brick wallpaper.

Out on the lawn he decides
he loves me and unbuttons
me down to the navel.

I puncture the plastic
and a waterfall of translucent
lids spills down the counter.

Spring shimmies through
the mini-blind slats. Yellow
paint blotches all our cottons.

Letitia Trent

We carry it everywhere.

The smell is clean, it's true,
but also mean. And also sour.

Eric Gelsinger

Walk to LaSalle Park

All day I've waited for the night,
As bad-ass mad hatters tip the upper sky,
Zoological zodiacal ambrosia, star shapes twist
My made-up constellations gyre and
Writhe, pigeons on wires and streetlights'
Interstate telegraphs withe birds' flight, turnpikes
Withy steel and, over, fireworks below: Fourth of July.
Rattling interstate bridge: coign of eye,
Telephone wiresight, the osier sky pregnant by night:
Great lake under the one moon, big pretty belly of a picnicker —
I stopped walking on the metal wicker
Bridge over I90 traffic turned river of lights, the loudest wind
Big-rigs screaming underneath give the bridge, my feet, my grip,
          a tingling.
Above, it starts to spritz, as mom would say, wetting bridge,
windshields, birds on wires, but I wait
To watch the woman's face reflect the redden fireworks.

Alice B. Fogel

Hearts

1. THE BOY

That night, it was full
like rainwater. They danced
but he wasn't sure how she felt.
All the small things
poured down. Having never flown,
never kissed anyone he didn't know
since birth, he forgot
the distances to lips,
forgot himself: the edges ran. All night
it seeped so anyone could see
the humid air. And still was full.
Who knew how like rain
it could spread and not adhere,
how his own shape could not
contain its weight, such heat, the vapor
like a living fog outreaching,
that the aching fullness
could loom so empty,
hunger with no mouth.

2. THE GIRL

Had it happened yet, what happened those times
she'd swear she heard the echoes
of slow pianos beyond the trees,
she would have remembered that then,
would have taken him there one day
as she later took the others and remembered this:
the first time another's heart struck
across the layered landscape of cloth

against hers, beneath it a vast open place spinning
within her waist's small circumference.
Not till much later would she recognize
that certain diffused focus familiar
when it drew from her as if by force
of one private gravity all the fluid
most often at rest inside. Even then
she was a well, but there was not yet a meadow
far up in the hills where finally the hammering
of untempered strings would fill her
with the liquid of impossible musical rain.

3. HEARTS

Had it happened that time it was full
of echoes like rainwater? They danced
to slow pianos, sure as trees.
All the small things remembered then
poured down, taken, one day flown.
He'd never kiss the others.
Since the first time birth's heart forgot
distance, lips' landscape
was her's: the edges of a vast, spinning night.
Within her, its circumference seeped
still, humid air, till much later
that rain—diffused, familiar, new—
adhered:
the gravity of private fluid shaped.
Inside: the wait, the rest, contained. Vapor evening
the meadow she was. They reached into a well
achingly full of a far hammering.
They strung their loom, emptied and tempered,
over the mouth of music's liquid hunger.

Carly Sachs

Ultra Violet

She remembered that he grew violets
under the fluorescent lights in the cellar.
It was the 1970's.
She wore pants.
He was dying.

That night she made eggplant, no
aubergine, the color of bruises,
the way they popped up
when least expected.
Their small heads watching her.
They reminded her of birds.

She pinned an orchid behind her ear.
Not the memory of it,
the way they grew in those trees in Florida,
she couldn't remember their name.
To be tucked in and woven around

twilight, incandescent
purple nights.
She was melting.
Was it cerebrum or
cerebellum?
She remembered only
that he grew violets.

Dean Gorman

The New New Instinctivism

the poor are dressed in noble-looking bath towels
no color exaggerated   hats   the stirring mystery
blotted out   Algerian blue you see
for 25 or 30 dollars my man is Sir Victor Sassoon
in your letter of the 15th you say such chaotic things

I was committing a sin today   had my typewriter
the gorgeous shoulder line you are playing on me
I was committing a sin you innocent-looking punk
my talent wasted on trash   you theatre of 1931

but the sense of life these days   the climate
the flirty quality my whole life is centered in you
I like looking for something big to result   and Tuesday
be prepared to be raped talking to me
naturally   I have been a crazy dreamer

I'm unplussed incidentally
are these low rolling hills this thing sad, classic
are these low rolling hills this thing sad, classic, laying you
in a fishing village   being dead is old, old looking
I remember Jung is one of them
Hannibal, Burlesque, Eduardo, American Express
one jerk who hasn't begun to fuck yet

let's prepare a daring mixture: put on
my watery black   you smashing 2 shots butcher-red
our friendship was exaggerated
really good   no color

Dean Gorman

imagine it all sad, classic   some provincial town
some people   not a sound of music
the country really sacred
it will break you whole in the face my love

Erin M. Bertram

[Love Poem: Watering Hole]

Because a few drinks does negative damage
to the soul. Call it praxis. Call it alibi.
Whatever the cost, the season's shock & alter,
you find yourself in one of the following quadrants
at one of the following angles:

  a) Lurched over a gin gimlet in khakis & a tie,
     last call three minutes & counting.
  b) Your cousin's graduation party, punch-spiked
     & dangerous, reciting Keats, the dark, dark bird
     perched & smiling on your shoulder.
  c)

When I walked through them (the double-doors,
the fifth & vital chamber), the waitress asked my
poison, brought it my way on a silver platter.
I remember you, fingering your empty glass.
But what we need breaks the skin & spills over
the lip. God has nothing to do with it. Do the math.
The sacral, the diurnal, the sacred, the dead.
We met in that secret room, made a pact, traded gestures.

I'd come home that night to find blood on my lip.
You'd wake the next morning in sweat, taste mint & metal.
I had wanted to make clear to you the velvet within.
The black smoke, the contour of fire. To describe
to you a world, the world, to you. Is what I mean.

Lea Graham

Crush 49

A space must be maintained or desire ends.
Anne Carson, "The Reach"

about your knees he whispered

above the hough, above the tongue

across some palm

after evaporation, lacey & leaf-like

against oil derricks, the dark undazzle

along the avenue, hair toss & fuck all

among a scumbling of colors

around, glittering with joy

at the table : *you're beautiful   you're beautiful   pass me the pepper*

before I go

behind the dunes

below the belt

beneath alabaster, vitrified

beside himself

between sacrum & ilium

by gum

110

down river

during gibbous moons

except Vienna & Paris

for this poem

from the 12 strings to my heart

in rough sheets three times or more

in auricles, in airports

inside the stall beneath

instead of a kiss

into the south of it

like her petunias & cosmos

near(er) he said

of moustache to helix

off the charts

on the lawn, paler than condoms' gleam

on top of her nightstand

onto the next thing

out of chants & variation

Lea Graham

outside windows, that entering takes away

over & over & over (again)

past Arcturus

since Cooley came to town

through corners we dance

to Halsted & Taylor

towards geometry

under enormous pressure of circumstance

underneath, yes, underneath

until April is

up Lisa Lane

upon learning "My Foolish Heart"

with him not there—

within ear's hive

without him—   she hears him, she sees

My Uncommon Concubine

My uncommon concubine misexplains pain for I misremember his printed face for ease and translation.

My uncommon concubine looks a wince in need of a gesture all his own.

My uncommon concubine piles haphazardly, piles nickel-plated steel, piles words in occasional lumps and gusts and he's a bit more difficult than the average concubine and I could cure him of all stiffness, if only he read my words.

My uncommon concubine is my pupil and instructor and holds my door and sends me his bills.

My uncommon concubine is not my gigolo.

I have no say over his undergarments.

I say, *You're not finished. Keep at it.*

I say, *How about another? How about you be quiet? How about you run to the store for strawberries?*

My uncommon concubine is intelligent. For a concubine.

I never discuss my love for my uncommon concubine.

I have much love for my uncommon concubine.

Question to uncommon concubine: Is it desire or disdain you hide with silence?

Reb Livingston

Statement to uncommon concubine: You are my uncommon concubine and you are intact and I could cure you of your sex-doll status with knitting needles and Christmas cotton.

Admonishment to uncommon concubine: You tend to repeat yourself; repetition is something you do often.

Conciliation to uncommon concubine: I'd promote you to full-fledged spouse.

If only it was allowed.

David B. Goldstein

What Lucy Used to Be

What Lucy used to be, I now am. Or rather, I accommodate her foibles; they live on in me now that she is gone. For instance: the thin switch of the horse's tail. The barn before sunrise, cold as oats. Trepidation in a nearby thrush. We believe that the dust layering theindoor ring comes from somewhere close by.

After the damage show, during which Lucy won a pink ribbon, we headed to the Amsterdam Pub to celebrate. Lucy still had on her dressage silencer. I was then just one of her admirers. My only claim to fame was having come up with a slogan for the owls in our local forest: Stronger than Ever! But from that, I was very famous.

I suppose she liked my girlish charm, my keychain of boys. She held the reins absently while the horses grazed in a nearby paddock. Later, on the roof of the next-door ranch house, we exchanged lockets. When we had sex, it was not exactly life, but more like the Cambridge Companion to Life, with essays of incisive brevity.

I have learned several lessons from my affair with Lucy: One: I know no Lucy who does not know me. Two: I am a gentle consumer. Three: I would like this bed to be free of stones if possible, and will defend the morning for it. Four: It is better to be a cabinet maker. Five: When the town doesn't want me anymore, it will say so.

Jason Bredle

You Can't Spell Slaughter Without Laughter

They filmed a movie about us in Montreal.
In the movie it was October, leaves the color

of blood. In the movie I cleansed my eyelids
with baby shampoo, I lied down with women

who sang national anthems at professional
football games and I thought only of you.

In the movie I ate moon cake and the vegetable
for which no human name exists,

I saw an ostrich bite a guy in the nuts.
He was the boom mike operator,

Tim, and he did not heed the repeated warnings
of the ostrich keeper. In the movie heretics decried

the erection of our God statue. The boom mike
operator, Tim, iced his swollen nuts.

In the movie the leaves were dyed with blood, October
was filmed in July. In the movie we spun ourselves

everywhere under the red leaves. I was really

happy and though you were on medication
I think you were happy too.

Allison's Guess

One time (maybe
it was for my birthday),
a couple—friends
of ours—brought over
some sorbet for
after dinner. The game,
for Allison and I,
was to guess the flavor.
So I took my time.
Had a couple of spoon-
fulls. Let each melt
slowly over my tongue.
I considered the
color and the fact that
whatever flavor it
was, it certainly had to
be more difficult
than *pink grapefruit*. I
even took more
time than I needed,
prolonging the
contemplative silence.
This would be
a crowning achievement.
"Blood Orange,"
I said, knowing I'd won.
I love that about
myself, how good I am
at guessing. How
bad I am at guessing.
How little it
matters to everyone else.

Anthony Robinson

September Improvisations

Because it was clear wide summer
everything was open: magnolias bigger than air,
the usual night sky, the Circle-K,
the legs of the woman who promised
to love you, which really meant "I won't
leave just yet…"

*

It was all clutter and fumble, flesh un-
hinging, the overhang, the window,
also open. It was September,
which means back to school sales,
which means the hazelnut tree will
drop its bounty.

*

It was two tongues, speaking out
of turn, out of sincere appreciation,
out of an earnest belief in art: the sounds
they made meant that they knew:
we all become artists, we enter
the creative field to get laid.

*

You who are not an artist, you who
haven't kissed anyone since
before the last windstorm, you who
paint the most beautiful blues and greens
can't imagine what I mean. But of course
you can. I've two tickets but I only need one.

*

She is not really like anyone, but again,
she's like every she before. He's an old
hand at summer romance, sea shore,
flubs. Together they have this: coffee,
the same quiet sense of humor. They met
at a convenience store. She bought a Slurpee.

*

These lines are unruly; they get away
from me. The end of the summer
used to mean pumpkins and smoke
in the air. Now it means something
like silence. The cold air no longer
consoles, isn't crisp.

*

These bodies are dirty. A spider
hangs suspended between the asphalt curb
and the high branch of a tree. In this dusk,
it looks as if it's hovering. Don't jostle
the limb. Don't undo the work of the heart here,
it'll get there on its own.

*

"I hope their mouths are open,"
"Give me wine, give me shoes, or a cigarette,
something, Darling. Something."
"I have a bauble. I have a book about devils."
"If you kiss me, I'll read your palm."
"It will be like looking at an eclipse."

Margot Schilpp

Declensions

I am the cases of Latin
leaning into you, past caring
how the patterns of birds' migrations

and the definition of synecdoche
might mingle in the realms
of higher thought, so give

the meanings back to me: the body
turning its pages in the dark,
the skin at ease in its temptations.

Does it matter that circles
describe the erotic notes
my body hears when anyone

says anything and your name,
that this world is a boa constrictor,
closing its mind on appetite,

and save for my ribs, the whole
of me would be a pulpy mass,
instead of just the center

of your rhythm? I even adore
when the inclinations are off—
when I am squeezed everywhere,

when I am touched and believe
that seeing is another kind
of gesture—irrational sight

using the breath, the bone,
these cells that sing together
and in tune all night.

The world declares to you: reason
is the method to survive,
and I can't deny reason,

although its thrall is fading
into and under my muscles
and the legs I wrap around you—

your flesh and my astonishing
willingness joined
in this clearest, coldest night.

Sandra Beasley

The Risk

Each year sixteen people are crushed by vending machines.

A lightning bolt can travel eighty feet underground, then strike.

Experts coat the blade in camellia oil before they swallow it.

When you come inside me it is yes   yes   yes   yes

and always your hands then gathering my quiet body because

no matter what pill, what latex precaution, you know I lie here

calculating the odds. *Across skin. Through cotton. Under water.*

You think I fear the belly's swell as a cavern not yet ventured,

this love a rope you can weave thick enough to hold us both.

But I know the depth of this particular dark. *When they reopen*

mine shafts, the canary goes in first to check for monoxide.

In 5 out of every 1,000, the whole uterus has to be removed.

I could sing of how thin the scalpel was, the comforting wax

of a Dixie cup. The sun was shining when I went in. Fact is,

sun was shining when I came out. No need for you to pull strings.

A private collector holds the last known sample of smallpox.

That flowing silk scarf? Can catch in the wheel of a car.

Grapefruit, if you're on Hismanal, will attack your heart.

Spelunk. Scuba. Marry. So anxious to play grownup games—

shaking the magic eight-ball until our future is buried in air.

Bruce Covey

Sense & Intersection

& in this one, I'm reading & sleepy, yes,
& you circle around me, around the house's rooms
busy & anticipating, looking for tasks that need completing

& why don't you sit & read or we could watch a movie
or cards or write something pretty alongside or walk

we decide to wallpaper a room, tearing out the old yellow flowers &
replacing them with new & deliberate yellow & level & plumb
      & afterwards
the room warm & wrapping now is something really to sleep in

& we do, circling the precise & detailed diaphanous geometry
      of sleep
ensuring all of these strings of numbers are irrational, amaranthine,
yet remain within the confines of today's inscrutable simplicity

Sleep Porn

Wanting sleep
Not like "Yes, please, I'd like
some lemon in my Coke" but
more like "Give it to me, give it
to me, give it to me, I
have to have it."

The caress of the mattress
the softness, firmness, just right
shape of the bed, feel of the pillow—

My eyes are already closing
and I'm in it, I'm there.

The Split Ends of My Beard Have Split Ends

My natural instincts are hardly ever right. When I sleep there is a voice in my ear coming through a cheerleader's megaphone in a really bizarre language. I understand fully. The world is out the window. When we wake on the weekends and my wife wants sex, I say *the furniture is feline, let's just snuggle.* Then I get up to pee. Nothing's as good as you think it is. I'm old enough now to say of my past, *that was a different time, I am a different person.* What was that noise? Successful ideas spring from great people. There is this music I heard once and if I could just have it with me at all times, there's no telling what I'd do. I'd like very much to speak the way I'm spoken to when I sleep, to have the perfect cheer. I'd also like to live forever among the brilliant colored cups of the tulips, but know how likely that isn't. If you want my advice, get out while you still can.

Nicole Steinberg

My Dick Strikes Twice in New York

Broadway is a tall,
noir corridor
of nylon & press-on
nails. Every high-
heeled girl belongs
to someone. Both times,
I am not offered coffee.
Every doorman sneers &
I cab it back to the hotel,
just in time for the end
of the continental
breakfast.

Elisa Gabbert

The Dream Because Love Ends

The person I'm playing tennis with keeps changing
back and forth between my brother and my ex-boyfriend—

I hope this means nothing; I just miss them both;
they make me feel fucking horrible. Some part of me knows

it's 4 a.m. and I'm too weak to dive for a shot; my racket strings
are on the verge of snapping gloriously like Achilles' tendons.

Allen wears the face from when we went apt. hunting
and he called all the places in our price range Calcutta.

As soon as I think of that flying roaches enter from the west.
My brother whacks at them with his old Wilson

as they whiz by our ears at their disgusting frequencies,
speed skating black figure 8's against the dusty sky.

We make a run for the Pro Shop and soon enough
we're drinking orange soda on the couch like everything is OK;

Allen drapes one of his long arms, his Hong-Kong-brown arms,
piano-hand arms, road-hockey-scarred-elbow arms

across my shoulder and says that everything is OK. On TV
they're showing footage from the courts and it seems like

we're still out there: Man vs. Nature. I wonder out loud
if it's some kind of joke and one of them says *If it is,*

it's the saddest, the longest, the slowest, most beautiful joke
you could tell. He doubles me over. He knows me so well.

Fear in the Reveal

Revisal, all. You, behind the tree. Come out with your hands up.
Away from the soup. Not a finger. No sling shots or anything from
the hip without warning.

You, up in swarms. Away from the hive. No pretending
hibernation.

You with the stylized hair, the red highlights, though you dodged
yellows in school and gladly go through them at corners. Bating
fate, you say.

Hey you with the coup. You fully loaded. You hit by the book
and carrying a bullet-proof one, you think, even though you don't.
Not thoroughly. One load is another's unload. Full remains empty
though you boast about the flood. At least be sure the latch is
locked, the fuse long enough.

You who refuse choice.

You who won't eye you in the look. Who takes and takes and takes.
Your corrosive strife is illegally parked, the tires flat, ire pooling on
the ground.

You buried your fear in a neighbor's yard and readily trespass
despite signs of detour and arrows toward joy. I'm miserably sorry
about your sorrows. You're miles from home and left your mind on
broil.

You with the plaster. You holding your breath for ransom. You
without the contours. Step away to step inside. Slip past. One foot
at a time. One space. Once upon a.

Alex Smith

Our Life is a Comic Book

I was wearing an ascot
made from a pillowcase
and following you around

like a lost dog,
and you were
so the girl

in the "Thriller" video,
and I was so the Michael
Jackson in that moment.

I was editing you
as I drank,
your face

washed out like
water on chalk,
and your lines

tightened and spoke
to me in the fashion

of those fantastic
portraits of birds

from the Audubon
books.

All I had to do was breathe
to get high, and you

kissed me and blew
into me a sweet,
sorrowful gel.

It filled me to the brim.
Sweat sunk
the back of my t-shirt.

Saliva grew
in the depths
of my mouth

and years passed
this way.

Now I'm drinking

Gatorade
with you in the garden,
my ascot

on tight,
and asking you:
"Will you marry me?"

And you just say,
"This moment,"
and you're crying,

and you say,
"I cannot forget this moment."

And I say,
"Why the hell
are you crying?"

Jill Alexander Essbaum

The Assignation

Tonight, she will dream of him
in sequences. How the sharp, slim

cut of his well-tailored suit
sliced like a knife through a very ripe fruit

the final share of her resolve
into twin, bitter halves. How tall

he stood against her, pestle-ing
the mortar of her pelvis.

And how the air, tight with disaster,
thinned to a stratospheric

black. She will dream of her maneuvers
and his rocket. How she flipped him like a lever,

how he plugged into her socket.
How he strangled her waist with the corset

of his straitjacket hands. How she surged
with urgencies

so adamant and so Jezebel,
he all but shrieked. How he took out her tortoiseshell

combs with his teeth. How she undid his buttons,
slid down his briefs, and feasted like a glutton

two feet above his knees. How the cloister
of her thighs wept liturgies and hours,

but how white and well worth it were the tremors and the woe.
And how his bliss, succinct as snow,

won her over. And she will dream, then, of his eyes, the pair of them.
How they thawed the ice of her arms like paraffin

beneath a lit wick's flame.
And the way

he unloosed with his stare
that knotty nest of hair

below her belly, above her pout.
And how it all *went down*

clumsily, like a sophomore poet's go at anapest.
How he fumbled up the ample of her breast,

but how oh how that only made her ardor
puff and swell. As well, how she quivered

like new brandy in a crystal glass.
And how—*and alas*—

the bright of afternoon
bent too soonly

into shadow, and how the droll, drab blue
of the rented room

relented when the night came on.
And how they put their clothes back on

slowly, lolling over each fasten.
How she'd planned to tell her husband

she'd gone shopping,
stopping

at three distinct boutiques before she found
that one, flesh-toned wraparound

for which she had been pining
(*and how that wasn't outright lying*).

And how against the setting of the TV's busted static
her husband had said *"That's nice."* And how he'd meant it.

Isotope

The dream where we can breathe together underwater
interrupted by the train again, scraping against the tracks
like a heartbeat dragging its chain. When he finally

comes over, he has a glass of milk on the porch.
He refused to come over for so long, and when he does,
he looks clean and shorn. Not stiff, exactly, but tucked.

All husbands are compromises, I thought.
Does anyone's body fall into anyone else's that way?
In the dream we are wrapped tightly; we inhale

each other's breath. I point out the bougainvillea.
He says, *that's crepe myrtle,* so I tell him about the dream
where the Spanish lady tore the flowers from our hanging plant.

I tried to make her stop. I'm just married, and it's raining
sweet ozone and wilting tulip centerpieces. I'm just
married and everything hovers and leans like

unfortified knickknacks. The man on the porch is not
my husband. We are fused vertebrae that float
in a moment of possibility. We do not become

unstrung. On the news they used to announce levels
of Strontium 90 in the milk each night—extremely reactive,
holding promise for use. The train, as always,

rattles like ocean with loose screws. It's not the same
as anything you can think of, and the rain beats it back.
How did we get to this place? (*Put your finger*

Erika Meitner

to my lips.) The dream that they switched the ceremony
location at the last minute and no one could find it.
It took so long to get here. The dream where I promised

we could go there on the train and I wouldn't leave you.
I dressed myself in white. Tonight the milk is glowing
with latent radiation. He asks, *What kind of milk is that?*

J. Marcus Weekley

Because My Flight Got Cancelled, The Clouds Above The Ocean Look Bluer

and I want to call my last girlfriend, no, boyfriend, and ask him out
on a date in Houston to an oyster bar where all the waitresses wear
pink hats and call the customers Ma'am and Sir. But we don't go to
the oyster bar, because he's got a show opening tonight and wouldn't
you know, I'm the star. I forgot all about it. My mother happens to
be in the audience—she's been hanging out with these girls from
work, and she brings me petunias after everybody in the audience
leaves. And my girlfriend is there, it's like a dream, and she tells
me how her day totally sucked because she tried to get a cab to the
airport to say goodbye to me, but then this totally skinny dude in
a wig and a tux shoved her out of the way with his umbrella—she
barely made it unscathed—and another friend of ours, from
Denton, just got married and do I want to come to the wedding?
Sure. I'll do anything once. So she asks me to be the best man and
I'm thinking this is the groom's job, but hey, who am I to question
tradition, and she fits me for a tux and invites me to dinner with her
dad, who I haven't met before. This is getting serious, I'm thinking,
and I'm not sure I'm ready to marry a girl who will buy crepe paper
just because she loves the smell of it, not to mention the texture, and
I'm eager to get out of the restaurant, it's the oyster restaurant by
gosh, the one Tom and I were supposed to eat at, and my fiancée,
now she's my fiancée, doesn't know that I dated Tom, but she knows
about George II. Man, I'm exhausted, so we go back to my place
and talk and drink sex-on-the-beach and watch the news about a
mountain range forest fire. All the ice melting must be like heaven.

Donald Illich

Another Foothold

My guide tells me
another safe foothold
is one length away,
but it may as well be miles.
My shoe's a baby rattle,
it shakes over the canyon
and its swooping vultures.

This is a dream.
I'm scaling a cliff
I'd never think of climbing.
Since I was 8
and my dad mimicked
my cries and moans
about going up
a glass elevator 7 floors,
I've imagined
being atop skyscrapers
or hang gliding
over the sea,
but I've always fallen,
landed,
then dropped again.

So, I know how
this trip will end:
a place to step breaks
under my weight,
my hands scratch
at walls that won't
slow me down.
I'm an inverse of sky,
a dark field

Donald Illich

of human-shaped stars,
each one crashing
without a last wish.

When I continue
struggling upward,
my breaths even out
rather than speed up.
I'm shocked into peace.
Hitting the peak,
I spot you below,
feeding whispers to deer,
yelling at hungry bears
to behave.

It's too far down
for you to hear me.
I want to shout
I'm all right,
I don't need you.
My lungs
don't give me enough
air to speak –
you're fading into woods,
part of a lush fern,
a sprig of wild berries,
beautiful things
I can't see from here.

William Allegrezza

distances
for lori

across darkened expanses where dolphins reign
counters cry the numbers to sleep
across   specious words lined along arches that
bloom   water itself   is new
across space that expands   with images of tubers
in growth is light falling from eyes forming circles
across two moments of here in place and
stumbling forward   you subtle beautiful alive

Michael Quattrone

February

Imagine, if you must, another man;
he'll imagine me. I'll touch you
with his foreign hands; you'll feel he
is sweeter, softer. I'll feel strange
inside you as a stranger; you will feel
better with another for your lover.
I'll imagine you, your usual mouth;
your tongue will be unusual between
his different lips. I'll feel your kiss
as an offense; he'll punish your
perversity, but I will come
to your defense. Then you will come
to his: that criminal whose fingerprints,
blushing on your breast, resemble mine.

Core of Affections

the future is here

in another reality   the choking begging
reality   the soft porn deformed
filling cracks   with   a   human   ocean
consumed   in   a   single   serving
etceteras   and bleeding cockroach
consumption   breathless and again
the future is here   again and again
the picture is mad   gnaws at the self
confronting a wall of oncoming traffic
mercenaries   with habitual disregard
for things and bodies   a sensation
rekindled in filth   line the causeways to
a choking point

a minute ago   swallowed by
a slow inward mute   demonic world
countless crawling faces   unable to speak
sheared off at the lips   a deflected
possible   a mathematical probable
a bride to a new moral code   in another
reality   already here

Cynthia Arrieu-King

Regimen of Bouncing Back

It was when I ran and ran towards that small white disk as if to
        catch it
It was when my friends slowly and without my knowing
        had changed
from lion-ugly strangers—
the kind whom you're real sorry are at your party—
to the people I had known my whole life and who had known
the whole sorry toothpaste fiasco.

I trapped up emotional dirty shirts and stared at the one true thing
        I could do
which became several,
which became impossible to ignore and not do:
couldn't I take down the laundry? And faster than that?

Impossible to dirty more.

I asked all the people I had been in running love with
did they love me, and one by one they said *I got a girlfriend, uh*

which caused me to feel pitiful and brutalized on the hotel rug for
        12 seconds
until I noticed another who said, *I love you but not so much in
        words as in the way*
small leaves, greenish, complicated by reproductive tubing
can only wave in the air and wave through fear

which caused me to feel argument and lack of illumination—
that one moment you must allow yourself to touch down into
        the purple disappointment
the touch surprisingly restorative.

Conspiratory Love Poem Addressing All Imaginable Possibilities

Two people in different boroughs could not survive
putting their heads together at one time,
such plans require feet and chests and hips;
these also have to get together or get near,
so everything ends up an ardent mess on an evening pier.

Arms can move a head, that's the trouble;
feet argue constantly with other feet
and treat the ground poorly.
Pretty soon it's Friday night,
and there are a bunch of people together making people.

Oh, horrible conspiracies! Oh summer sun groping down
into New Jersey! Spare us the periods and the condoms,
the commas and prosthetics; those two people necking
in the park are committing luxurious crime after crime!
She is a wheelbarrow; he is a wheelchair.

Ah, a little paranoia is a comfortable thing; a lot of
that sex is only what people do with their pets,
and on the return of steady breath sensuality is no longer
a bad witch in a pleather-sticky dress.

So I walked freely around with the slanted clouds
floating Uptown; my lightning was unzipped,
but on my way to meet you I realized that there was fog
all over my notion, so I perspired into Daybreak:
Northern Hemis-Fire.

Betsy Wheeler

Non Sonnet for Telling You Everything

Like how high banjo trills make me go electric.
Like how charity. Like how gold.
Like I'd like to take you in and feed you a little
sweet milk. Like you'd mind, but I'm, like,
so tired of honesty like California fault lines.
Like how this is the big moment. The time of it
& I'm ready now for the next time.
Like how cuteness rules the dating quadrants.
Like how sexy. Like when I say you look good
in white linen I mean sheets. Like I'd like to
rob your booty bank. Like how I'd take my
winnings to the grave.

Susan Denning

Down at the Heels in the Ditch

Give me a snowstorm, get me a hat.
We need weather and boots to walk in,

we need the moon and an unholy din
to keep us in curtains and fish. All that

we want is waterproof fabric and coins
to keep us counting and clutched. Your chin

looks quiverish and sad. Where have you been? We knew
the way but the binoculars burst, the compass was crushed.

The trees can't invent us—they're unsigned and undreamed,
they're cloudstruck and squirreled. The ground is a scene,

a wish. The sky rambles sockless. Give me your gloves
and fetch me a stove, crouch sweetly with me and wonder:

where is the roof of the house we should live in?
what is the name of that bird in your mouth?

Rebecca Loudon

don't you feel it's dangerous to want while losing
time hurry hurry

sweet and pungent your body having spilled
your shaved neck raw
the wasp crawls deeper into the fig
my tips swollen with it

today the bird census came to my house
to find the kingfisher's errant nest
I did not entice them though I feel criminal
like my second husband whose name I stole
he of the golden body hair quiet as a pet
I won't get over it   he left a welt

my house drowns with sex
I crawl naked toward you on the floor
white and dark meat the dark
full of blood

I ask to be blindfolded
you smell like grass
and charred steak
with lemon pepper   on a gold charger
a new evangelism

paris the genius cat is in the yard stalking the bird
his heart clapping so fast
it's become   its own animal

Sedna Becomes Inuit Goddess of the Sea: a Prequel

A seabird has promised you
a stinking nest of bearskins and fish.
You have no choice in who you love.
If you try to leave, father will put you in a canoe,
shove you overboard. He will cut your fingers
if you hold on to the lip; he will smack you
with his oar. Live for him: on old fish food,
and what you can make from your fingers.
When your hands ache, don't punish
the carp and hagfish with sickness and storms.
Live on for him: in your house of whale rib and
ground, your one good leg always bent beneath
a caldron of boiling seals.
Old woman, forgive the sea,
let the people starve.

Evie Shockley

initiation

i love you was the first lie. or call it
a pillow: a soft place for me to lie

to myself, cushioning a fall. you red
my violet: blues scene through rose-

colored dialogue. action. hope takes
flight. novelty masks malfunction.

wishing coats skin and gestures like
a film. the second story: *this might hurt.*

power is a tool i hand over. *might* as
a noun in a poorly conjugated truth.

am

staccato engine of the heart. rush forward towards the other end of a wire, previously molten glass or what was once a button and a can. this vibration stands in for the center, vacant kingdom or distant receiver. one that stands for foreclosure. turn down covers, torn honeysuckle drop.

as a child i could whimper. as a woman, stand alone. it's difficult to move forward against obvious tracings. harder still to stand and bear, digress is something like please relent. to be off any fixed articulation tells the arteries to contract. a small red heat that amplifies with time. a static discharge, unequivocal shock. ally yourself with the momentary blaze, a significant odor. burned from fingertip to the outermost reach, pleading with the dew of the body, a weighty signification.

a design: from this perspective, a small, three-legged cat in the street transmits minute attention, a shed hair, hunger. you mention force fields and i automatically think plexiglass or the deep bruise that doesn't discolor. push hands, softly.

AnnMarie Eldon

henged

saved for whenever he could or would
rather than being areas of day-to-day activity
fact that their ditches were located inside their banks
indicated that they would have been used

in a defensive function
if it got serious and that the barrier
their earthworks provided was and is more likely to have been
functional rather than
    symbolic

not like flags nor even emblems but family matters
and private and different for each of them
according to no formal
conjectured that whatever he took to be

inside his enclosures was intended to be separate
from the outside world
and perhaps only known to select individuals
or groups; this alignment a contentious

issue. Popular belief that theirs towards certain heavenly bodies
in fact orientation highly invariable
and more determined by local topology
armchairs and such rather than any

desire for spiritual orientation
a slight tendency for having an entrance
set in the north or north-west quarter smile
identified following no statistical analysis only gut-

full whilst generally their axes aligned approximately south east to
north west or northone
twosouth west but who could care
less
authorities argue but none to look

up
none to reference on this particular no
go. Structures used as declinometers
used to measure positions of rising or setting
often considerably post-

dated, themselves off the back foot and not necessarily
connected and certainly not necessarily connecting
conjectured that they could have been synchronized
yet planting doubts

or timing unshared religious rituals poles

apart
stones would indicate

during whilst others appeared
framed certain markers so that nearby others
do not mark nor do not interfere nor do not with such observations
finally placed at particular

lassitudes a number where the same two indicated she
this time rising and setting away from
for both the spring in his garden
and the spring in her step

frightened her with its unaccussédtomed courage
henges she learned from
and was present from the extreme north to the extreme south of her
body

AnnMarie Eldon

so her departure could not
have been of greater
impor
stance

Anne Gorrick

The May Garden

A   That calcium moon
                      passes in and out of clouds
nightmare   bleached with impatience
                      If the rest of the sky
                      dark purple and caustically
                      then a leather garden
in   The green delivers chrome plate
                      a nightmare in enamel
                      I can sit inside it later and tremble
enamel   when August blows hotly across my skin

Kissed at the end of night, one side ached
A Stangl jug filled with lilacs
white with nuances
The azaleas are dark crimson and spiky
as if they carry in their casual hands
high boots in black patent leather
A garden to send nightmares that come in chromium and lacquer
The heliotrope is vanilla smeared, a consolation prize

                      I have more installations
                      that must be carried out this weekend
floating   The stone sink to the shade garden
                      must be planted with impatience
in   rose and blank under heavily nuanced shade
                      Must celebrate "Colette" around the azaleas
the   I want a black garden someday, a leaning garden
                      an S&M garden
river   A garden to send nightmares that come floating
                      off the river

This calcium month of cloud entrances and exits
Rather you should place this weekend within me

Anne Gorrick

There are many plants
their irritation shiny in pink and white
As for me "of garden; Black"
The fact that a garden often desires plants
a garden that sends the unpleasant impression of command
Dignity passes from one sector of my skin into another
I am possible to tremble
As a reward of comfort, you move into shade

Digital   Where is that side of night that smells like
                   Stangl filled with
                   lilacs, achingly?
in their   This is the calcium month, cloudcover
                   Digital in their magenta, "Pink Delight;" Hole
magenta   It is a black starting with a shovel
                   That it establishes, the facts want me in leather

I consider the house an extremity
the focal point of a lateral night
Difference and puncture cross my skin
In ardors of azalea, wildness arisen
The night will often load blackness onto another color
Dignity passes for the hot suction of our skins

An   The fucking as a form of extremity
                   across the lateral night
                   Stangl lilac-white achingly
irritation   Then I went back into the house
                   urged largely by a slow night of fucking
                   A weekend went wrong inside me
that   Foxgloves seemed to be numbered individually
                   another joy in pink, in buddleia, in
                   self-deprecation
                   An irritation that shines in pink and white
                   under heavy shade

shines   A consolation prize in this vanilla scented
                                          heaven

That time in me went toward the house
Cloud wild, ragged days into rags
The garden will be black someday
and I will send in the nightmare: chrome and lacquer

Gina Myers

A Model Year

The ground shifts but no one notices the spinning.
No one notices the stoplight or the time I said no.

Three years' time folds into a single instant.
Structures rebuild themselves & everyone moves forward.

Always wanting what we can't have, we create tension
one word at a time. Pulling the narrative away until we're lost

& it's lost, left behind in the restaurant or on the subway.
The little bird in the tree rebuilds its nest, the cat

watches through the window, wanting. Always wanting
what we can't afford, some leisure time or a casual hello.

Attempting to fill an empty space with any thing:
yesterday's news, photographs, a box of buttons &

loose thread. Trying to keep my eyes open after a bad dream.
Don't let me fall again. There's only so much a body can take

but still stupid desire. To attempt a composition, a theory
of migration. Hands gathered in the lap, syntax folding

in the mouth. This testament to a year, a document
of your travels. Something to fill the space.

*

Something to fill space but still the body waits.
Attention shifts & fills itself with birds in the distance,

a car horn, children throwing rocks in the street.
In the distance, an echo. Thought interrupted by

phone lines. To create structure out of broken pavement,
a cup of coffee or any welcoming thing. Move forward

without hurt. Build your day around re-setting the clocks:
rise & fall & compile a new grocery list.

Sweep the floor on Sundays. It's easy to fall in a dream.
Easy to confuse foolishness for generosity, a bathtub

for a sensory deprivation tank. One day you wake
& everything has changed. Time has erased so much,

taking from you all the people you once loved.
Each movement becomes measured, how

you reach for the change in your pocket.
It's easy for the body to peel after it has been burned.

Easy to push forward & no one will notice
how you reach for change & the leaves turn.

*

No one will notice when you fall. The ground
shifts & the pavement catches up with you, meets

your chin. And when it happens, the body ages.
Ten years pass but you think instead of youth.

Afternoons spent dirty & riding bikes, tin cans
tied to tree branches. Where once there was a we

there is now an I, an imagined you.
Where once there was a witness to distance,

time folds into an envelope. I am trying to step
outside the body, for the body to push forward, always.

To take a command & go without injury. As if
following orders were as easy as brushing your teeth

or any domestic thing. To make a space for one's self.
The cat asleep in the window. A new set of silverware,

pictures to frame for the walls. Comfort in the most tedious
of things. A way to make the time pass.

*

A way to make the time pass is as good as any
validation, any idea of happiness, opening

a new book, finding solace in preparing dinner.
Moving to L.A. or Toronto has never been

the answer. The home we built made sense
if only for a brief time. The dream in which I'm falling

& startle myself awake has always been here.
I couldn't watch the images on tv, bodies

hurtling through space. Push inside yourself.
Paint the living room orange.

Buy new curtains to block out the sun. When
you didn't have to go to work, you slept,

filled whole days with sleep. Waking to eat,
smoke a cigarette, have a drink. It's easy to fall

for a dream. Easy to pretend the flowers are blooming
specifically for you, or the walk home a yellow brick road.

Attempt to make sense of wanting, make sense
of the empty seat across the table.

*

Moving has never been the answer but always
an understandable response to the empty seat

across the table. Threads come loose & the button
needs to be re-sewn. Time to trade sweaters

for short sleeves. The sun on the skin acting
as an agent of love to keep you golden & warm.

To hold you in memory golden & warm.
An afternoon nap in the park. The body continues

to grow, moves forward, guarded.
Memory like loose thread unravels, rebuilds,

constructs a new sequence of events.
Remembered faces that were never there, never

a part of this story. Forgive me if I repeat,
I don't know where else to go.

No new words to explain my appearance here today.
No new words for today & waking & sleeping.

Gina Myers

I've attempted to re-trace my steps,
looked the last place I was.

*

Re-trace & re-learn. Return home to the daily
tasks, making pasta in the kitchen the heat

is inescapable. Bare feet flat against wood
floor & it's still two months till August.

The neighborhood is heating up,
more bodies on the street

each day. More voices till the early hours
of the morning. Broken streetlights &

the train passing overhead. Impossible to drink
the glass of water while it's still cold.

When standing in the door of the refrigerator
isn't enough. When the promise of fall &

the return of jackets is not enough. Another year
passes & the body is tired. Falling into a dream,

an escape from monthly bills & worries
of money & debt. When I last dreamed of you,

there was a hole in your side. A fist-sized hole.
I reached for you & reached my hand right through.

*

The act of reaching for another causes
such misery that it's easy to forget the good.

164

The memory of New Year's replaced
with the memory of packing boxes.

Every new failure returns to this. The ground shifts
& everything goes on without you, without me.

A car runs a red light & strikes a child on a bike.
The cat licks his claws clean having satisfied

his urge to hunt. The tape rewinds & begins again.
The question of how long things can go on this way

is answered with always, of course.
Always. I know this but still can't stop.

*

There are no rules for this. Things are easier
when there's a code of behavior. Waiting

for Saturday to pass into Sunday & Sunday
into the work week so one knows what to do

with their time. Language neither the problem
nor the cure, just something to occupy myself with.

No one taught me the softness of the quilt
against my cheek. It was something I could only

learn myself. No one taught me how to deal
with emotion. How to handle restless nights.

And so I lied when I said I didn't know how
I got here: a series of bad mistakes & misjudgments.

Gina Myers

A touch of idealism. Hope then disappointment.
Really I've traveled nowhere. Standing in the same place

for three years. Still wearing the same blue jeans,
only now a hole in the knee.

*

After three years, the skin is a little thicker.
Bruises have come & gone. The body moves

between sickness & health, slips between sheets
each night. There may be new scars, a story for each.

It's easy to pretend nothing exists outside
your four corners, your own little concerns.

Easy to turn off the tv & not read the papers.
It's easier not to make decisions but to just allow

things to happen, hereby escaping any culpability.
Blame it on bad luck & not bad decisions.

A blank page can mean a fresh start or nothing
to say. This line of thought will continue &

I can map its progress, using tacks & colored string.
It's easy to pretend that I'm the only one who feels

this way, or feels anything so acutely. Confusing
one's self for the center of the world, & then

news of a death in the family, a roadside bomb, &
protesters killed by their government shatters everything.

*

The shattering of everything has become a way
of life. The ground shifts, no one notices.

It's wrong to make either one of us out as criminals.
It's wrong to fill this longing with a haircut

& new shoes. Wrong when we run into each other
on the street to pretend no hurt exists or offer

a casual hello. There are no rules, no guide
to get through the day. Always wanting

what we can't have, the attempts
to make sense of it have failed.

Days progress & add up & the calendar changes.
We pour a new cup of coffee, cover ourselves

with new blankets, separately. The sun shifts
through the window & the cat sleeps, his leg twitches.

It's easy to close my eyes & think of falling. Easy to feel
the body collapse on the bed, the mattress rushing to meet you.

A Man & A Woman

He proposed to her in Pompeii, where in a cluster of silver wings they found a man and a woman boned in each other's arms. He carried her into Rome in falling blue and white. A gypsy was stealing the coins out of the fountain. But, no matter— they danced in the streets and kissed in the square and as they finally stumbled into the hotel at dawn he started on about the bodies. In the stomach of a shark, he said. Can you believe it: a man, woman and child all reduced to bones in the stomach of a shark. She laughed and she played with her hair and she slammed the headboard against the wall.

Seance, 1858

*Based on a photograph from the exhibit "The
Perfect Medium: Photography and the
Occult," Metropolitan Museum of Art, New
York, 2005.*

The room was dark, my heart
was pumping, we sat in a circle,
men and women, there were
people I didn't know.
I was proud
of my new shoes, I was
the prettiest one, and the medium
sat me by her side.
It was dark, the room
in shadows. We sat
in a circle, our hands
touching. The medium spoke softly, I
leaned in to hear her,
she was saying the dead
were in the room with us,
their presence was strong.
I felt breathless, dizzy,
I didn't want to miss it. There was rustling,
was it the dead? The medium
tensed, the black
curtain parted, it was dark,
but I saw it, white, with hair,
and the medium placed
my hand on it. My heart tipped
on its axis, I wanted to pull away
but she held my wrist. I
was confused, dizzy,
it was dark in the room.
What was it? I thought

Kim Roberts

it might be a man, it felt fleshy,
it might be his manhood,
I screamed and let go, I upset
my chair. Another woman
screamed too, I heard furniture
moving, low voices, confusion.
I wanted to touch it again.
I reached out my hand
but the curtain had closed,
the medium was talking,
she was trying to calm us, she said
an ectoplasm was very rare.
The dead were near, we were
lucky, she said, very lucky.
Suddenly it was over, we were leaving.
What was it? I was young,
embarrassed, a little angry.
My heart was so loud in my ears.
I didn't feel lucky. My shoes
were too tight. Did I seek
the spirit and touch only flesh?
Or was I so afraid of the flesh
that I chased away the spirit?
I could feel on my wrist
where she had held me
the traces of her warmth
seeping away.

Erin M. Bertram

[This Is About Making Love]

This (unlike others, & for various reasons) is about making love.
This (is like flying, is like pulling wings off a fly, stroking its back all
the while) is about making love. This (you are uncomfortable, sex
equated with pulling wings off a fly, stroking its back all the while)
is about making love. This (though, does not much deflate your
already blooming heart) is about making love. This (why all this
talk of equating, making, flying, pulling, stroking) is about making
love. This (have I, subject composing subject, equated or merely
juxtaposed) is about making love. This (you'd rather pull your own
hair, click off your sins) is about making love. This (I don't blame
you) is about making love. This (dear reader) is about making love.
This (rear up, gentler side face-out, split the juxtaposed) is about
making love. This (tie up, lathe down, wander like the river raging
you are) is about making love. This (mixed metaphor in tow) is
about making love. This (keep the wings intact, keep the wings
intact) is about making love.

Simon Perchik

*

So rounded a season :the sky
in a few hours, fits
and the moon has a warmth
a harvest —your breasts
overnight —from your heart
everywhere a flickering light
flies open and the moon
heated, already noon

—streams widen from stone to stone
as if this floor still had a secret spot
and voices differ from one another
—you say the dry stones are innocent
the rest venomous, to listen for stones

for the thickening :each stream, you say
and turn toward my lips
—you lift my head as if some star
was falling, only once
and I had to know how it feels
to drown, to be a season
to wait for daylight, to wait
for evening and slowly turn.

Nathan Hoks

Life Drawing

She is so naked it's like an obstacle course. The
house is for sale, we can't find our way
out to the front door. O sure, it's good
to be that naked when you have all day and sunlight,
when the skin resists the urge to leap,
keeps quick to the touch, minds its business
in the hay where horses meet to nibble on things
and sometimes each other. O sure, horses,
rub it in. If I am lucky I will untie
the knot my hose is in and drench everything
I see, woman, man and child, the whole shebang.
The werewolf can't believe I'm saying this
but I don't believe in him so we're even
and night can continue winding along the freeway
out of town. Which it doesn't, it just sits there
hovering over us like we're dead spiders
waiting to be swept away and we wonder what
it means to be swept away. The rock juts out
and trips me. As I'm leaning on my hand I look
at the ant colony. They are naked naked naked
and the only one who minds is me.

Joseph Bradshaw

from The Way Birds Become

with my feathers entangled in your navel
and then a place where there are holes
a bird's glazed eye's as white as its flight.
I see you see that you can only see
a bird from the outside
but have you ever glimpsed beneath
the cloudy exterior? Once plumage is stripped
it reveals almost nothing about skin
but everything about itch.

Hugh Behm-Steinberg

Night and Day/ Birds Again

Staying up late, wearing headphones, being poor.   But not tired,
       you are spread out   and you want to.   Your mom says
              until you were named   you filled up space
       but you weren't anyone   and you were very hard to see.
              The ocean, full of fish,   held onto you too,
          little swimmer.   Ships moved above you slowly
with their cargo and their crew.   Divinity pervades
                     even the slightest of acts.

       Therefore such radiance,   with light pollen on
              your upper lip and   smoke in your purse,
and the saltwater marsh,   tidal pools, and you   see birds again
       you let yourself see   birds again   and your mind
       lets the birds in   and the music   starts when they come.

Adam Fieled

fish

more spring than spring. curtains
had a seemingly yellow presence.
there was trembling & vulnerable.
there were martial fish between us.
a bovine moon hung congruent.
the mystery was all in what's simple.
there was a calling, but not by us.
we weren't talking, but springing.
all the fish had solid skeletons.

had the cards been shuffled differently. had they

Theodore Worozbyt

Birthday Poem

I sat down
to write
a book for you.

It was to start
with an essay
about onions.

I would tell
everything: Copra,
Nocturne, Pearl,

all the names,
seeds dark and trim
as periods

at the end
of homely rounded
sentences. Better

this: Pull them
up when they wither—
onions cure

in moving air;
they sweeten, in time,
in the sun.

Derek Pollard

An Elegy for the Innumerable

Q: *Is it ever enough*

A: Spill of seltzer into cut glass

     Fog overwhelming the Golden Gate Bridge

Q: _____

A: Outside the window half a dozen magpies scatter two by two

     Gentle clink of glasses in the kitchen sink

Q: *A bright summer morning*

A: In the living room, the bed we have slept in

     Now piled with pillows, sheets lying on the floor

When we draw open the blinds, jet trails crisscross the sky

     Over there, love. Look. And there

Ka-Boom: A Translation of Sappho

[The words in brackets are supplied by conjecture]

The [man—Cuban cigar affixed] to [his fat lip—burns
        in a Hebridean burr]

that [enhances the woman's lush heterodoxies.]
        Their [sheepdog will va[r]nish

into English court painting] but [today he's pleased
        to pant and spit]. The [sun

is] the [color of piss in a blue basin.] The [sunbeams
        have baked their mottled skin

into Bakelite. As] Aphrodite [spins acetates
        of Bollywood-style jazz

they rise from the ottoman] like [tapeworms] and [dance
        the peppermint Totentanz].

Allyson Salazar

Hide

Orange peel
pith
under nails
lifts nails
and skin
together
citrus cuticles
bite

Cream coat
on morning fruit
skims fat
slices of
slippery lips
sucking

Screaming skin
in bed
a face I peel
bite
suck slip
is not you
coming.

Jen Tynes

Charged As It Is Called

Negative capability means
two boys riding a locomotive can
fall in love with their headphones
on. Paper, rubber,

silk, porcelain and other
carefully chosen things rattle
but cannot be given

an audience without desire,
and the mountain breaks also

have no woman-born gong
and hammer, cannot list back
and forth their needs.

Electricity made the dead frogs'
legs move. I demand that satisfaction
also come to terms with me,
this triplet standing

in line for the powder
keg who is no longer attracted
to each other but touches
them. Similarly a room

must change, go hot to become
worth knocking its lights out
for. If I am standing in

for the headphones and
the engine goes who
are all the songs about.

John Sakkis

from Rude Girl

as in the feet of jesus were washed by smaller hands/ eroica. the
wood can collect a black film only on the bottoms of feet. lifting
himself the knobs of his ankles flatten. the new wood becomes
support into the carriage/ cross-braced-(carpenter's term.) said "and
that a kelson of the creation is love." he heard the song/ the sang
enclosure of barn wood. and rain would make the bay seat wet the
wind where coming to/ string-piece used to keep a load in place.

two men/ one woman/
too looking two men/ woman
not talk/ one woman
walking isn't silver mitsubishi/

THE POET

"sometime you aren't get what you deserve."

"their neutral the footage for the product."

the lung becomes what starving child would eat

the lung running in dreams
without stopping better than flying,
run-down in front, there
seemed to be woods and water
the scrimed light made
tunnel vision in—actual.

-the mettlesome action of the blood horse-

(ergo)

John Sakkis

POET(ESS)

3. Two ministrel-show dances: the first slow and
shuffling, the second fast and frenetic.

        when we danced upon the sea-shore
        we went to the old grave
        how many of us looked upon
        a sea-foam on the wave

9. Waterfowl with soft feathers

in a speech on divorce...
some the pre/ un-occupation
of things (bowery,
steeple, other)

becoming the non-self,

becoming what is to do,
etc.

-the bicycle man
could be found
there too.

Jim Kober

Problems with this Moment and the Last

We're in the car when the hotel calls
to say the antique telephone is missing.

Return it at once or accept the $170 lean
on the credit card.

You swear you know nothing. I swear.

Before this weekend
I thought we were convinced
leaving solves everything,

but it's the drowsy bleach light of the hotel lobby
cooperating with the information

of how you move
that says you barely relate to yourself
let alone my ambition
still short of dual beam headlights.

Now when I go out
                I leave my hands with no one.

It had an ear receiver. It was a voice to base unit.
I didn't use it. Maybe you did. If so, who'd you call?

Intentions snared between reaction and the right set of yes.
No reason to administer any dose of feeling.

Even the least selfish eel will lend half its body
to electrical production. I turn the car around, lose my way,
                and you find it charming.

Bottle of Chianti

Feeling as sweetly dissipated as. His eyelashes were the only thing to catch the light. Evening disintegrated from there. Nothing I say in Italian as real as the same said in English. He used both my balled-up towel and the stuffed duck for a pillow, but I didn't want them back. Anything I asked was like tossing a match. Around the corner, they give you free bunches of basil, rosemary, and bay leaves. But at 5am it rained so hard it woke me.

Eric Abbott

Port Authority

Suss in cant comes
clean, plums glutton,
unsung tongues, singed.

Go blind child slow
into any new harbor.
Every disaster is mined.
Every mine somebody's sister.
Every artery somebody's dumpster.

I neither despair
nor presume, I am.
Nothing within me
makes me wrong.

Smock of filth, smut
bath, Dis-dress, in submersion
savvy is the trick.

Bridal shower, daughter
shrine, altar piece, what
of it. As bride-to-be,
showered in wet sequins,
who could love a beaten man, who
could be beneath me now.

Silverfish swim in our correspondences,
firebrats in others' heated exchanges.
Littlest sentients, life sentence, commutable drive.

Eric Abbott

This spill, albatross, necklace
of Hylas, of man having passed, whimsy all over
her splashy accessories, a wake, diamonds
extracted from coal ridge, move mountains
to get the goods, downhill, everything
finds its way here, finale with fireworks.

The definition of quest: endless
attempts to get back to that
undivided, liquid existence, crawling
from the water, the ditch, the crotch
into the garbage, the grail, the grave.

Say no to cave painting.
Some things we love for other
than what they are, for what
they aren't. If felching salvation, missionary,
position yourself before a friendlier door.

White Fingers Scissoring a Love Poem into Snow

Dear Coworker, I refuse to write another poem where the moon glints like a hubcap lost in a retention pond. My morning glass of milk casts a spell that keeps it perpetually upright. It's dazzling and empty. When I put my head down, the pines make a muffled song of the wind. I substitute because syntax once mattered. Example A: The doors of perception vs. the perception of doors. Example B: I haven't forgotten your mouth—no ordinary winter—your mouth, which gives fruit a gender. And your teeth, how they collapse the skin of your daily apple—never green, never yellow—only the red an other could love. And yet—yet I hesitate a taste. I am so very uninsured. The scaffolding of your arms appears entirely accidental.

Mathias Svalina

Blackberries

How did we survive?
They say the new paint does not match the old paint.
After the accident, the beds of nails.
After the blackberries, a lacewing fly.

They say the gas masks
were hidden in the berry patch.
The chokedamp floated
from the mine's mouth.

Was the chokedamp equal
to the toad's dead eyes?
Was the lacewing fly?
Was the lacrimator?

The blackberry sap
is impermeable,
is a gelatin of neon.
Go to it. We must finish this boredom.

Nevertheless

Let's have another drink,
I don't feel like
Moving yet she said and ordered
As he'd been there the day before

When she saw him walk away
She wanted to call
But didn't there was
No space for voices

Nevertheless
He heard her
Searched for her

That was why
She stayed
Just in case

Passing the dark during evening spaces

Impact of bar lighting on digital photo Photo
screened on his cellphone To the phone he
presses her numbers Her number one reason is
his number one desire Is that desire? Or control?
Control yourself she thinks The sentence goes
on as lines of ink implicate other details What
she thinks to him it matters

A man in the act of love A man in the way of
presence that to be taken pleasured want, fell into
push of pure fall Wind-scattered fragments free
the occlusions Hands to grab for leaves circling
their trees in the swirl Your mouth, she had her
desire, swallowing His hunger, tasting her touch
his broken fast, dominion

Jill Alexander Essbaum

The Men We Marry, the Men We Fuck

This one kissed me beneath the stars.
That one fondled me up the stairs.

This one confessed his sins but to God.
That one demanded his pity aloud.

This one drove me to the store.
That one drove me like a car.

This one gave me violets and asters.
That one brought me violence and disaster.

This one wed me in the chapel.
That one ate me like an apple,

And he was as handsome as he was doomed.
Lovely as lust, but fickle as the moon.

This one built a house to live in.
That one fed me glass and poison.

This one tended and kindled hearth.
That one threw me to the dirt

And by the greenbrier patch we tangled,
Hand to thigh and lip to nipple.

The men we marry, the men we fuck:
This one doubly filled my cup,

That one used me up.

Contributors

Eric Abbott was the University of Arizona Poetry Center Summer Resident in 2005. His poems have appeared in *American Letters & Commentary, Spinning Jenny, Skanky Possum, Born, Goodfoot, Word For Word* and *Spork*. He lives in Missoula, Montana with his wife and their two dogs. He doesn't usually refer to himself in the third person.

Deborah Ager's writing has appeared in *The Georgia Review, New Letters, Best New Poets 2006,* and elsewhere. She has been awarded fellowships to the MacDowell Colony and the Virginia Center for the Creative Arts. She's the publisher and editor of *32 Poems* (http://www.32poems.com). Her book of poems, *Midnight Voices,* will be published in March 2009 by WordTech Press.

Malaika King Albrecht poems have recently been or are forthcoming in several magazines and anthologies, such as *Kakalak 2007: An Anthology of Carolina Poets, Pebble Lake Review, The Pedestal Magazine, Shampoo,* and *Mannequin Envy*. She has taught creative writing to sexual abuse/assault survivors and to addicts and alcoholics in therapy groups and also is a volunteer poet in local schools. Her manuscript *Never the Same River* was a semi finalist in the Seventh Annual Elixir Press Poetry Awards, and her poem "Magician's Assistant" won the 2007 Poetry Southeast Poetry Contest.

William Allegrezza teaches and writes from his base in Chicago. His poems, articles, and reviews have been published in several countries, including the U.S., Holland, Finland, the Czech Republic, and Australia, and are available in many online journals. Also, he is the editor of *moria* (http://www.moriapoetry.com), a journal dedicated to experimental poetry and poetics, and the editor-in-chief of Cracked Slab Books (http://crackedslabbooks. com). His chapbooks, e-books, and books include *Lingo, The Vicious*

Bunny Translations, Covering Over, Temporal Nomads, Ladders in July, Ishmael Among the Bushes, Fragile Replacements, and *In the Weaver's Valley.*

Molly Arden is the co-editor of *No Tell Motel.* Several translations from Catullus with her commentary are forthcoming in *Classic Literature in Translation.* She blogs at http://mollyardensaysso. blogspot.com.

Cynthia Arrieu-King is a doctoral candidate at the University of Cincinnati and an echocardiographer. Her chapbook, *The Small Anything City,* is available from Dream Horse Press. Her poems have or will appear this year in *Copper Nickel, RealPoetik,* and *Boxcar Poetry Review.* While she admits the goetta is good in Ohio, Kentucky is still home.

Robyn Art is a native of Lincoln, Massachusetts. She is the author of *The Stunt Double In Winter* (Dusie, 2007), a text-visual collaboration with the artist Robin Barcus, entitled, *Dear American Love Child, Yours, The Beautiful Undead* (Dancing Girl Press, 2008), *Degrees of Being There* (Boneworld Press, 2003), *No Longer A Blonde* (Boneworld Press, 2007) *Vestigial Portions of the Dead Sea Scrolls* (Dancing Girl Press, 2006) the text/visual collaboration *Scenes From The Body* (Dancing Girl Press, 2007) and the online chapbooks *The Last Time I Saw Bonnie Blue* and *Body The Non-Body* (ensemblejourine.com) Currently she can be found living in Brooklyn with her daughter, Titania.

Sandra Beasley won the 2007 New Issues Poetry Prize for her book *Theories of Falling,* selected by Marie Howe. Her poems have also been featured on Verse Daily and in *Best New Poets 2005.* She lives in Washington, D.C., where she serves on the editorial staff of *The American Scholar.*

Hugh Behm-Steinberg is the author of *Shy Green Fields* (No Tell Books, 2007). His poetry has appeared in such places as *CROWD,*

VeRT, Volt, Spork, Slope, Dirt, Swerve, Zeek, Cue, Aught and *Fence*.
He teaches in the graduate writing program at California College of
the Arts where he edits the journal *Eleven Eleven*.

Aaron Belz writes poetry in his hometown of St. Louis, Missouri.
His work has appeared in *Boston Review, Fence, Painted Bride
Quarterly, Black Clock*, and other places, and his first full-length
book, *The Bird Hoverer*, was published by BlazeVOX in 2007.
Another of his manuscripts, *Clementines*, was selected as a runner-
up for the 2006 Marsh Hawk Press contest by Denise Duhamel.

Erin M. Bertram is a fellow and instructor in the MFA Writing
Program at Washington University in St. Louis, where she edits
shadowbox press. Her work has appeared or is forthcoming in
Bloom, Columbia Poetry Review, CutBank, Knockout, and *Best New
Poets 2007*, & an interview with poet Rebecca Wee is forthcoming
in *Lyric Poetry Review*. She is the author of three chapbooks:
Alluvium (dancing girl press, 2007), *Here, Hunger* (NeO Pepper
Press, 2007) with Sarah Lilius, and *Body Of Water* (Thorngate
Road, forthcoming), which won the 2007 Frank O'Hara Award.

Mary Biddinger teaches poetry writing and literature at The
University of Akron, and serves on the faculty of the NEOMFA.
Her poems have appeared or are forthcoming in a variety of journals
including *Crazyhorse, The Iowa Review, Notre Dame Review*, and
Ploughshares, and her first book is *Prairie Fever* (Steel Toe Books
2007). She is Founding Editor of the literary magazine *Barn Owl
Review*.

Ana Bozicevic-Bowling emigrated to New York from Croatia in
1997, and has since written in English. She is the author of two
chapbooks: *Morning News* (Kitchen Press, 2006) and *Document*
(Octopus Books, forthcoming). Find her recent poems in *Octopus
Magazine, The New York Quarterly, the Denver Quarterly, Absent,
Saltgrass, In Posse* and the Outside Voices' 2008 *Anthology of Younger
Poets*. She coedits *RealPoetik* and works at PEN American Center in

New York City.

Timothy Bradford's poems have appeared in *Bombay Gin, Crossconnect, Diagram, H_NGM_N, Redactions, Runes,* and *Softblow,* among other journals. He authored the introduction to *Sadhus* (Cuerpos Pintados, 2003), and in 2005, he received the Koret Foundation's Young Writer on Jewish Themes Award for his novel-in-progress, based on the history of the Vélodrome d'Hiver in Paris.

Joseph Bradshaw is the author of *The Way Birds Become* (Weather Press, 2007), and *This Ocean* (Cannibal Press, forthcoming 2008). His poems and prose have appeared in *Denver Quarterly, Jacket, No Tell Motel, Tarpaulin Sky, the tiny,* and other journals. He probably lives in Portland, Oregon.

Jason Bredle is the author of *Standing in Line for the Beast,* winner of the 2006 New Issues Poetry Prize, and *A Twelve Step Guide,* winner of the 2004 New Michigan Press Chapbook Contest. He lives in Chicago.

Jenny Browne is a James Michener Fellow in Poetry at the University of Texas and the author of *Glass* (Pecan Grove, 2000) and *At Once* (University of Tampa, 2003). She lives in downtown San Antonio in an estrogen heavy house full of two female pets, two female children and one tired man.

Jenna Cardinale is the author of *Journals* (Whole Coconut, 2006), a series of collage poems. She lives in New York, where she teaches poetry writing at Lehman College.

Bruce Covey is Lecturer of Creative Writing at Emory University and author of three collections of poems—most recently, *Ten Pins, Ten Frames* (Front Room, Ann Arbor) and *Elapsing Speedway Organism* (No Tell Books, Reston, VA). His poems also appear or are forthcoming in *Aufgabe, Verse, LIT, The Hat, Bombay Gin, Boog*

City, 580 Split, and other journals. He edits the web-based poetry magazine *Coconut* and curates the What's New in Poetry reading series in Atlanta.

Phil Crippen was born in Syracuse, New York and now lives in Phoenix, Arizona with his son Philip. He attended both the University of Arizona, and The University of Oxford in England. Phil is the Director of Information Technology at The Heard Museum. Recent work has appeared in *Shampoo Poetry, The Argotist Online, MIRAGE/PERIOD(ICAL), Face Time,* and *Eoagh.* Phil maintains a blog called, "stamped and metered flying fish," located at http://pkcrippen.blogspot.com.

Susan Denning has had poems recently in *Rattle, Pindledyboz* and *Perihelion.* She lives with her family in Portland, Oregon, and edits the online magazine *Caffeine Destiny.*

Michelle Detorie lives in Goleta, CA where she tutors writing and works with rescued seabirds. She edits *WOMB* poetry and Hex Presse. Her poems have appeared in *How2, Foursquare, Typo,* and elsewhere. A chapbook, *DAPHNMOANCY,* was published by Peter Ganick's Small Chapbook Project and another chapbook, *Bellum Letters,* was published as part of the Dusie Chapbook Kollektiv. A third chapbook, *A Coincidence of Wants,* was recently published by Dos Press. Visit her online: http://www.daphnomancy.com.

Laurel K. Dodge lives and writes in northeast Ohio.

Mark DuCharme is the author of three collections of poetry: *Cosmopolitan Tremble* (Pavement Saw Press, 2002); *Infinity Subsections* (Meeting Eyes Bindery, 2004); and most recently, *The Sensory Cabinet,* published in 2007 by BlazeVOX Books. The latest of his several chapbooks is *The Crowd Poems* (Potato Clock Editions, 2007). He has taught in Naropa University's Summer Writing Program and at Front Range Community College. "Poem" is part of a writing project titled *Inappropriate Content*, other parts of which have appeared or are forthcoming in *Fascicle, Hamilton Stone Review, Milk Magazine, Talisman, Vanitas* and elsewhere.

Peg Duthie works as a copyeditor in Nashville, Tennessee. Her writing has appeared in *Clean Sheets, Rhymes for Adults, Strange Horizons*, and elsewhere, as well as in the inaugural *Bedside Guide*.

kari edwards (1954-2006) received one of Small Press Traffic's books of the year awards (2004), New Langton Art's Bay Area Award in literature (2002); and is author of *having been blue for charity* (Blazevox, 2007), *obedience* (Factory School, 2005), *iduna* (O Books, 2003), *a day in the life of p.* , (subpress collective 2002), *a diaryof lies* (Belladonna Books, 2002), and *post/(pink)* (Scarlet Press, 2000). edwards' work can also be found in *The Best American Poetry 2004* (Scribner), *Bay Poetics*, (Faux Press, 2006), *Civil Disobediences: Poetics and Politics in Action* (Coffee House Press, 2004), *Biting the Error: writers explore narrative* (Coach House, 2004), and *Bisexuality and Transgenderism: InterSEXions of the Others* (Hawoth Press, Inc., 2004).

AnnMarie Eldon, an identical twin, evolved from cryptophasic origins in once densely industrialised Birmingham, England. She was taught by her gypsy grandmother to say the alphabet backwards before the age of three. Juggling various personae interiorae, children and hormones and practicing counter-cultural reclusiveness, she achieves adult differentiation and spiritual equanimity within the mediocrity of a picturesque Oxfordshire market town.

Julie R. Enszer is a writer and lesbian activist living in Maryland. She has previously been published in *Iris: A Journal About Women, Room of One's Own, Long Shot, the Jewish Women's Literary Annual, and the Harrington Lesbian Literary Quarterly.* You can read more about her work and order her hand-made chapbook, *My Lesbian Herstory*, or her limited edition broadside, *When We Were*

Feminists, at her website, http://www.JulieREnszer.com. You can email her at JREnszer@aol.com.

Jill Alexander Essbaum's latest collection, *Harlot*, was published in October 2007 by No Tell Books.

Noah Falck teaches Language and Thought at Grafton Kennedy Elementary. He has published poems in *Bat City Review, LIT, Gulf Coast, Word For/Word, Pilot*, and *Absent*. Other portions of *Life As A Crossword Puzzle* have appeared in *H_NGM_N, Backwards City Review, Dusie, Can We Have Our Ball Back, CAB-NET, No Tell Motel*, and *Boog City*. His first chapbook, *Homemade Engines from a Dream*, is forthcoming from Pudding House.

Michael Farrell is completing a research M.A. at the University of Melbourne. He has published 3 books: *ode ode* (Salt, 2002); *BREAK ME OUCH - graphic poetry-* (3 Deep, 2006) and *a raiders guide* (Giramondo, 2007). He spent the winter of 2007/8 as an Asialink resident in Nagoya, Japan.

A Massachusetts native, **Katie Fesuk** is a 2006 Georgia Author of the Year Award nominee for her chapbook, *If Not an Apple* (La Vita Poetica Press), a doctoral student in English and Creative Writing at Georgia State University, and Poet in Residence at The Walker School. Poems can be found in *Slant, Apple Valley Review, Sea Stories, Chattahoochee Review, Water~Stone, Rock & Sling*, and *Atlanta Review*, among others.

Adam Fieled is a poet/musician based in Philadelphia. He is the author of two books: *Opera Bufa* (Otoliths, 2007) and *Beams* (Blazevox, 2007). In addition, he has released two chapbooks, *Posit* (Dusie Press) and *Funtime* (Funtime Press). His albums include *Darkyr Sooner* (mp3.com, 2000) and *Ardent* (WSG, 2004). He is currently a Ph.D. candidate at Temple University in Philadelphia.

Alice B. Fogel's third poetry collection, *Be That Empty*, appears in late 2007. She teaches writing and other arts, and creates one-of-a-kind "reprised" clothes for that unique ecological fashion statement (http://www.LyricCouture.com), while living off the grid with her family in NH.

Elisa Gabbert is an editor of *Absent*. Her recent poems have appeared or will appear in *Pleiades*, *Cannibal*, and *LIT*. A chapbook, *Thanks for Sending the Engine*, is available from Kitchen Press, and a book of collaborative poems written with Kathleen Rooney, *That Tiny Insane Voluptuousness*, is forthcoming from Otoliths Books.

Eric Gelsinger was born in Buffalo, NY in 1977. He studied physics, neuroscience, psychology, and history on a full scholarship at the University of Buffalo and graduated summa cum laude as Presidential and Distinguished Honors Scholar. In the last ten years, he has traveled to England, as a student at Oxford University, as well as to Europe, Guatemala, Cuba, and South America. Recently, he moved to New York, worked for the United Nations, and he now works as a US equities trader. He is a co-founder of House Press.

Scott Glassman is the author of *Exertions* (Cy Gist Press, 2006) and *Surface Tension* (Dusie, 2006) with Mackenzie Carignan. His poems have appeared or are forthcoming in *Jacket*, *580 Split*, *Iowa Review*, *Jubilat*, and others. He also co-curates the INVERSE Reading Series in Philadelphia.

David B. Goldstein is the author of the chapbook *Been Raw Diction* (Dusie, 2006), and his poetry has appeared or is forthcoming in numerous journals, including *Jubilat*, *Harp and Altar*, *Typo*, *Pinstripe Fedora*, *Epoch*, *Alice Blue Review*, *Dusie*, and *The Paris Review*. He teaches creative writing, Renaissance literature, and food studies at York University.

Dean Gorman lives in Portland, Oregon, and is a graduate of the Vermont College MFA Program in Writing. His poetry and prose has appeared or is forthcoming in *Forklift, Ohio, The Portland Mercury, No Tell Motel, Oregon Humanities, Octopus, Caffeine Destiny, Typo, Unpleasant Event Schedule*, and *Music Liberation Project*. He is co-editor of *Pilot* and Pilot Books and plays in the band Gas Lanyard.

Anne Gorrick's work has appeared in: *American Letters and Commentary, the Cortland Review, Dislocate, Fence, Goodfoot, Gutcult, Hunger, MiPOesias, No Tell Motel, The Seneca Review, Sulfur and word for/word*. Collaborating with artist Cynthia Winika, she recently produced a limited edition artists' book called *"Swans, the ice," she said* through the Women's Studio Workshop in Rosendale, NY. In addition to being a bookmaker, she also works in encaustic, printmaking and traditional Japanese papermaking. She lives in New York's Hudson Valley.

Lea Graham's poems, translations, reviews and articles have been published in or are forthcoming in journals such as *Notre Dame Review, American Letters & Commentary, Mudlark, Shadow Train* and *The Worcester Review*; her work was included in the recent anthology, *The City Visible: Chicago Poetry in the 21st Century*. Her chapbook, *Calendar Girls*, was published in spring of 2006 by above/ground Press in Ottawa. She is currently an Assistant Professor of English at Marist College in Poughkeepsie, New York, where she, otherwise, passes her time playing gin rummy, working on her triceps, and planning her next trip (the Galapagos!).

Kate Greenstreet is the author of *case sensitive* (Ahsahta Press, 2006) and three chapbooks, *Learning the Language* (Etherdome Press, 2005), *Rushes* (above/ground press, 2007) and *This is why I hurt you* (Lame House Press, 2007). Visit her online at http://kickingwind.com.

Piotr Gwiazda is the author of *Gagarin Street* (2005, Washington Writers' Publishing House). He teaches modern and contemporary poetry at the University of Maryland, Baltimore County.

Nathan Hoks' poems have recently appeared in *Crazyhorse, Octopus Magazine, Pilot Magazine, The Burnside Review, Court Green* and *CutBank*. He has received fellowships from the University of Iowa and the Vermont Studio Center. He lives and teaches in the Boston area.

Josh Hanson lives in Sheridan, Wyoming with his wife and children. He teaches writing to 7th graders and edits both *Eucalyptus: a journal of the broken narrative* and End & Shelf Press.

Shafer Hall is mighty proud to be a poet for Team No Tell. See also his No Tell book *Never Cry Woof.* Look for new Shafer Hall poems in *LUNGFULL!*

Donald Illich has published poetry in *The Iowa Review, Fourteen Hills, Passages North, No Tell Motel, Lit,* and *Cold Mountain Review.* His work will appear in future issues of *Nimrod, Combo, and The South Carolina Review.*

Salwa C. Jabado is a Miami native who lives in New York City. She received her MFA in Poetry from the New School, works in editorial at Fodor's Travel, and writes reviews for *Críticas Magazine* in her spare time. She is currently working on a novel in verse entitled *The Mechanicals.* Find out more at http://www.salwajabado.com.

Charles Jensen is the assistant director of the Virginia G. Piper Center for Creative Writing at Arizona State University. He holds an MFA in poetry from ASU and is currently pursuing a Master's degree in Nonprofit Leadership and Management. He is the author of three chapbooks, including *Living Things*, which won the 2006 Frank O'Hara chapbook award, and *The Strange Case of Maribel*

Dixon, which is forthcoming in fall 2007 from New Michigan Press. He was a recipient of a 2007 Artist's Project Grant from the Arizona Commission on the Arts. His poetry has appeared in *Bloom, The Journal, New England Review, spork*, and *West Branch*. He is the founding editor of the online poetry magazine *LOCUSPOINT*, which explores creative work on a city-by-city basis.

Ron Klassnik lives on a river and stares at a mountain a lot. One of his dogs is small and red, the other big and black. The red one's the Alpha. His poems have appeared in *The Mississippi Review, The North American Review, Sentence, Caesura, Pilot Poetry, MiPOesias, The Kennessaw Review, Front Porch* and other journals. Black Ocean Press will be releasing his first book *The Holy Land* in early 2008.

Jennifer L. Knox's second book of poems, *Drunk By Noon*, will be published in fall 2007 by Bloof Books. A new edition of first book, *A Gringo Like Me*, will also be published by Bloof Books in 2007. She is a three-time contributor to the *Best American Poetry* series, and is currently studying avian linguistics via correspondence.

Jim Kober has affection for his enemies. He lives in Tucson, Arizona.

Dorothee Lang edits the *BluePrintReview*, an experimental online journal, and is the author of *Masala Moments*, a travel novel about India. She lives in the South of Germany and takes regular trips through the real as well as the virtual world. Her work has appeared in *Pindeldyboz, Hobart, Eclectica, The Mississippi Review, Juked, Subtletea* and numerous other places. For more about her, visit her at http://blueprint21.de.

Sueyeun Juliette Lee grew up three miles from the CIA. Currently, she resides in Philadelphia, where she edits Corollary Press, a chapbook series devoted to new work by writers of color. Her chapbooks include *Perfect Villagers* (Octopus Books) and

Trespass Slightly In (Coconut). She can be reached at s.juliette.lee@ gmail.com.

David Lehman's most recent book of poems, *When a Woman Loves a Man*, came out in 2005 from Scribner. He is the editor of *The Oxford Book of American Poetry* (2006) and series editor of *The Best American Poetry*, which he founded in 1988.

Reb Livingston is the author of *Your Ten Favorite Words* (Coconut Books, 2007). Her poems have appeared or are forthcoming in *Best American Poetry 2006, The American Poetry Review, Caffeine Destiny, MiPOesias* and other publications. She's the editor of *No Tell Motel* and publisher of No Tell Books.

Rebecca Loudon is the author of *Tarantella* and *Radish King* (Ravenna Press), and *Navigate, Amelia Earhart's Letters Home* (No Tell Books.) Her third collection of poetry, *Cadaver Dogs*, is forthcoming from No Tell Books in summer 2008. She teaches violin to children.

Clay Matthews has recent work in *H_NGM_N, The Laurel Review, LIT, Court Green, Forklift, Ohio*, and elsewhere. He has two chapbooks: *Muffler* (H_NGM_N B_ _KS) and *Western Reruns* (End & Shelf Books), which is available for free online. His first book, *Superfecta*, is forthcoming from Ghost Road Press in 2008.

Justin Marks' latest chapbook is *[Summer insular]* (Horse Less Press, 2007). New poems appear in *Soft Targets* and are forthcoming from *Cannibal*, Outside Voices' 2008 *Anthology of Younger Poets*, and *Tarpaulin Sky*. He is the founder and Editor of Kitchen Press Chapbooks and lives in New York City.

Kristi Maxwell's poems have most recently appeared (or will soon appear) in *Forklift, Ohio, Practice*, and *Court Green*. She is the author of *Realm Sixty-four* (Ahsahta Press, 2008), and she currently studies and teaches at the Univeristy of Cincinnati.

Gary L. McDowell's poems have appeared recently or are forthcoming in *Ninth Letter, DIAGRAM, The Southeast Review, Bat City Review, No Tell Motel, RHINO, Copper Nickel, Memorious, Bateau, Pebble Lake Review,* and many others. He currently teaches Creative Writing at Western Michigan University where he is pursuing his Ph.D. He is the Assistant Poetry Editor at *Third Coast* and an editor at New Issues Press.

Dulce Maria Menendez aka **Didi** is a single mother of four. Many of her poems are about a Cuban thang. She also publishes a literary magazine or two.

Erika Meitner's first book, *Inventory at the All-Night Drugstore*, won the 2002 Anhinga Prize for Poetry, and was published by Anhinga Press in 2003. Her work has appeared most recently in *APR, Prairie Schooner,* and *Crab Orchard Review.* She is currently simultaneously an Assistant Professor of English at Virginia Tech, a doctoral student in Religious Studies at the University of Virginia, and a member of the *Virginia Quarterly Review's* Poetry Board.

Michael Meyerhofer's book, *Leaving Iowa*, won the Liam Rector First Book Award. He is also the author of three chapbooks— *Cardboard Urn, The Right Madness of Beggars,* and *Real Courage.* He has been the recipient of the James Wright Poetry Award, the Laureate Prize, and the Annie Finch Prize for Poetry. His work has appeared or is forthcoming in *Ploughshares, Arts & Letters, North American Review, Mid-American Review,* and *Green Mountains Review.*

Steve Mueske lives and writes in Minnesota, where he is the publisher of three candles press and curator for poetry365.com. His full-length collection, *A Mnemonic For Desire*, was released in 2006.

Gina Myers is the author of the chapbooks *Fear of the Knee Bending Backwards* (H_NGM_N 2006) and *Stanzas in Imitations* (New School 2007). She lives in Brooklyn where she co-edits *the tiny* with

Gabriella Torres.

Cheryl Pallant is writer and dancer whose books include *The Phrase, Into Stillness, Uncommon Grammar Cloth, Spontaneities*, and *Contact Improvisation*. She teaches writing, dance, and a blend of the two at the University of Richmond in Virginia.

Shann Palmer lives in Richmond, Virginia where she hosts poetry readings and workshops. She maintains a calendar at http://groups. msn.com/FlashPaperPoetry for events in Central Virginia.

Alison Pelegrin is the author of *Big Muddy River of Stars*, out from the University of Akron Press this fall, as well as *The Zydeco Tablets* (Word Press 2002) and three prize winning chapbooks, the most recent of which is *Squeezers* (Concrete Wolf 2005). The recipient of a creative writing fellowship from the NEA, her work has appeared in *Poetry, Ploughshares*, and frequently in *The Southern Review*. She lives in south Louisiana with her husband and their two young sons.

Simon Perchik is an attorney whose poems have appeared in *Partisan Review, The New Yorker, No Tell Motel* and elsewhere. Readers interested to learn more about him are invited to read the essay "Magic, Illusion and Other Realities" at http://www.geocities. com/simonthepoet which has a complete bibliography.

Derek Pollard currently teaches in the English Department at Syracuse University, where he is pursuing his Ph.D. He is an associate editor at New Issues Poetry & Prose, and a contributing editor at *Barrow Street*. His poems and reviews have appeared recently in *580 Split, American Book Review, Court Green, Diagram, Pleiades*, and *Word For/Word*, among others.

Cati Porter is associate contributing editor for *babel*, and founder & editor of *Poemeleon: A Journal of Poetry*. Her poems and book reviews have most recently appeared in *kaleidowhirl, LiteraryMama,* *mamazine, Mannequin Envy*, and *Poetry Southeast*, with more forthcoming in the anthologies *White Ink: Poems on Mothers and Mothering* (Demeter Press) and *Letters to the World* (Red Hen Press). She lives in Riverside, California, with her husband and two young sons.

Andrea Potos' full-length collection of poems *Yaya's Cloth* was recently published by Iris Press (http://irisbooks.com). She lives in Madison, Wisconsin. Her poems appear widely in journals and anthologies, including *Women's Review of Books, Atlanta Review, Poetry East, Southern Poetry Review*, and *Claiming the Spirit Within* (Beacon Press).

Poet and collagist/object maker **Laurie Price** is the author of *Except For Memory* (Pantograph Press), *Under the Sign of the House* (Detour), *The Assets* (Situations) and *Minim* (Faux Press). Her work has appeared in numerous print and online journals, including *Arshile, HOW2* (poetry & mixed media sections), *the east village* (poetry & art) *readme, MiPOesias, The Duplications, Barbara Henning's blogspot*, et al and is forthcoming in *Eoagh*. She's lived in many places across the US, Mexico, and Morocco, and now lives in Granada, Spain. A new collection, *Radio at Night*, is, ojala, forthcoming.

Michael Quattrone is a co-curator of the KGB poetry reading series in New York City, and the author of *Rhinoceroses* (New School Chapbook Series, 2007). His work appears online in journals like *Octopus, Jacket*, and *No Tell Motel*. He lives in Sleepy Hollow, New York, with his wife and three children.

Jessy Randall's unsatisfied lust for sleep began in 2001, when her first child was born. Ghost Road Press published her full-length collection of poems, *A Day in Boyland*, in 2007. Her website is http://personalwebs.coloradocollege.edu/~jrandall.

Kim Roberts is the author of two books of poems, most recently *The Kimnama* (Vrzhu Press, 2007). She is editor of the acclaimed online journal *Beltway Poetry Quarterly* (http://www.beltwaypoetry.com) and co-editor of the brand new *Delaware Poetry Review* (http://www.depoetry.com).

Anthony Robinson is the author of *Brief Weather & I Guess a Sort of Vision* (Pilot Books). He lives and works in Oregon.

Carly Sachs is the author of *the steam sequence*, which was the winner of the Washington Writers' Publishing House first book prize in 2006. She is currently an Arts Fellow at The Drisha Institute in New York City. With Reb Livingston, she curates Lolita and Gilda's Burlesque Poetry Hour.

John Sakkis's recent chapbooks include *The Moveable Ones* (Transmission Press), *Gary Gygax* (Cy Gist Press), *Rude Girl* (Duration Press) and *Post Bulletin* (TaxtPress). He lives and loves in the Lower Haight, SF.

Allyson Salazar is a mad potter who lives with her husband and two illiterate toddlers. She was a Jane Kenyon Scholar at Bennington College. A small bit of her work appears in an online anthology she co-edited with David Lehman titled, *FU: An Anthology of Fuck You Poems*, at http://www.slope.org.

Christine Scanlon was awarded the Barrow Street First Book Contest for her poetry collection *A Hat on the Bed*, published in 2005. She has a poem included in *Best American Poetry 2005* and has had work published in such journals as *Goodfoot*, *Barrow Street*, and *Comstock Review*.

Morgan Lucas Schuldt is the author of *Verge* (Parlor Press: Free Verse Editions, forthcoming fall, 2007) and *Otherhow* (Kitchten Press 2007), a chapbook. He lives in Tucson where he edits the literary journal *CUE*.

Margot Schilpp's books are *The World's Last Night* (2001) and *Laws of My Nature* (2005), both from Carnegie Mellon University Press. Poems have appeared in *Chelsea, The Southern Review, Shenandoah, Denver Quarterly, Hotel Amerika* and elsewhere. She is an editor for Tupelo Press, an independent literary publisher. She earned an MFA from the University of Utah, and lives in New Haven with her husband and daughter.

Patty Seyburn has published two books of poems: *Mechanical Cluster* (Ohio State University Press, 2002) and *Diasporadic* (Helicon Nine Editions, 1998). She is an assistant professor at California State University, Long Beach, and co-editor of *POOL: A Journal of Poetry*, based in Los Angeles.

Peter Shippy is the author of three books, most recently the novella-in-verse *How to Build the Ghost in Your Attic* (Rose Metal Press, 2007). Shippy has received fellowships in drama and poetry from the Massachusetts Cultural Council and the National Endowment for the Arts. His poems, plays, and essays have appeared in *The American Poetry Review, Harvard Review, Iowa Review,* and *Ploughshares.* He teaches literature and writing at Emerson College and lives in Jamaica Plain, MA with his wife and two daughters.

Evie Shockley is the author of two poetry collections: *The Gorgon Goddess* (2001) and *a half-red sea* (2006), both with Carolina Wren Press. Her work appears as well in numerous journals and anthologies. A Cave Canem fellow and the recipient of a residency at Hedgebrook retreat center for women writers, Shockley teaches African American literature and creative writing at Rutgers University, New Brunswick.

Alex Smith holds an MFA in poetry and fiction from the New School. His poems have appeared in *Octopus Magazine* and *Sink Review.* He is the editor-in-chief of *Red China Magazine* and a founding editor of the *Dick Pig Review.* He lives in Manhattan.

Nicole Steinberg is an editor of *LIT* and the Associate Editor of *BOMB Magazine*. She earned her MFA in poetry from The New School, and she curates and hosts the Earshot Reading Series, located in Brooklyn, New York.

Alison Stine is the author of *Lot of My Sister* (Kent State University Press, 2001). Her poems have appeared in *Poetry, The Paris Review, The Kenyon Review, The Antioch Review, The Beloit Poetry Journal, Swink, Tin House,* and others. Her awards include a Wallace Stegner Fellowship in Poetry. She lives with her very fun husband in New York.

Mathias Svalina lives in Lincoln Nebraska where he co-curates The Clean Part Reading Series & co-edits *Octopus Magazine* & Books. Poems of his have appeared in *jubilat, Fence, Typo* & *Denver Quarterly,* among other journals. His first chapbook is *Why I Am White* (Kitchen Press).

Erik Sweet was born in Buffalo, New York and currently lives in Albany. His poems have appeared in *MiPOesias, Jacket, Vanitas,* and other magazines. He co-edits *Tool a Magazine,* which can be found at http://www.toolamagazine.com.

Eileen R. Tabios has released 15 poetry collections, an art essay collection, a poetry essay/interview anthology, and a short story book. She most recently released the multi-genre collections *The Light Sang As It Left Your Eyes* (Marsh Hawk Press, New York, 2007) and *SILENCES: The Autobiography of Loss* (Blue Lion Books, 2007). She's also the editor of Galatea Resurrects (A Poetry Engagement) at http://galatearesurrects.blogspot.com.

Bronwen Tate is the author of a poetry chapbook, *Souvenirs,* (self-published 2007 as part of the Dusie Chapbook Kollektiv). Some recent poems have appeared (or are forthcoming) in *The Cultural Society, Foursquare, LIT,* and *How2*. She received an MFA in poetry from Brown University in 2006 and recently began a PhD program in Comparative Literature at Stanford University, where she is also poetry editor for *Mantis: A Journal of Poetry, Criticism & Translation*. She writes about reading, writing, knitting, and cooking (when not actually performing these activities) at http:// breadnjamforfrances.blogspot.com.

Molly Tenenbaum is the author of *Now* (Bear Star Press, 2007), *By a Thread* (Van West & Co, 2000) and of the chapbooks *Blue Willow, Old Voile,* and *Story;* her old-time banjo CD is *Instead of a Pony*. She lives in Seattle, teaching music in the living room and English at North Seattle Community College.

Chris Tonelli lives in the Boston area where he runs The So and So Series. He has work forthcoming in *Cannibal, H_NGM_N, Drunken Boat ,* and *Good Foot,* and poems of his will be included in Outside Voices' *The 2008 Anthology of Younger Poets*. His chapbook, *WIDE TREE: Short Poems,* is available from Kitchen Press, and *A Mule-Shaped Cloud,* a collaborative chapbook written with Sarah Bartlett, is due out from horse less press in January.

Letitia Trent lives in Brattleboro, Vermont. Her work has appeared in *The Denver Quarterly, Pebble Lake Review,* and *MiPOesias,* among others. She is a co-editor of *21 Stars Review*.

Jen Tynes lives in Denver, Colorado and edits horse less press. She is the author of the following books, chapbooks, and collaborations: *Found in Nature* (horse less press 2004), *The End Of Rude Handles* (Red Morning Press 2005), *The Ohio System* w/ Erika Howsare (Octopus Books 2006), *See Also Electric Light* (Dancing Girl Press 2007), and *Heron/Girlfriend* (Coconut Books, forthcoming 2008).

Ashley VanDoorn's poems can be found in the following journals: *American Letters & Commentary, The Canary, Seneca Review, WebConjunctions, Gulf Coast, Northwest Review, No Tell Motel, Typo, Coconut, Word For/Word, Shampoo, glitterpony,* and *La Petite Zine*. She currently lives in Atlanta, GA.

Fritz Ward's poems have appeared in or are forthcoming from *American Arts and Commentary, Swink, Salt Hill, Columbia, Diagram, The Journal, Small Spiral Notebook* and other fine publications. He holds an MFA in creative writing from the University of North Carolina Greensboro, where he served as a poetry editor for the *Greensboro Review*. He currently lives in Santa Rosa, California.

Born in Chattanooga, Tennessee, **J. Marcus Weekley** works at a food-serving establishment, and enjoys horror movies. His books include *from four years* (prose poems) and *Look Out Below and Other Tales* (stories) at http://www.lulu.com/whynottryitagain, not to mention the just-released *Texas Dance Halls* (he took the photos, Gail Folkins wrote the essays), out from Texas Tech University Press. Marcus is single, not really looking, though he appreciates a well-built ass (mostly male). You may view some of his images at http://www.flickr.com/photos/whynottryitagain2.

Betsy Wheeler's chapbook, *Start Here*, is forthcoming in fall 2007 from Small Anchor Press. Co-editor of *Pilot* and Pilot Books, she lives in Northampton, Massachusetts where she works for *Wondertime* magazine.

Theodore Worozbyt's first book is *The Dauber Wings* (Dream Horse Press, 2006). His second, *Letters of Transit*, won the 2007 Juniper Prize (University of Massachusetts Press, 2008). Recent work appears in *Poetry, Po&sie*, and *The Best American Poetry 2007*.

Kim Young is an MFA candidate in Poetry at Bennington College and a recipient of Bennington's Jane Kenyon Scholarship in poetry. Her work has recently appeared in *5am, Askew, POOL*, and *Pebble Lake Review*. Her poetry has been nominated for a Pushcart Prize and was a runner-up in the 2006 dA Center for the Arts poetry contest. A chapbook, *Divided Highway* is forthcoming from dancing girl press.

Also by No Tell Books

2008

Personations, by Karl Parker

Cadaver Dogs, by Rebecca Loudon

2007

Harlot, by Jill Alexander Essbaum

Never Cry Woof, by Shafer Hall

Shy Green Fields, by Hugh Behm-Steinberg

The Myth of the Simple Machines, by Laurel Snyder

2006

The Bedside Guide to No Tell Motel, editors Reb Livingston & Molly Arden

Elapsing Speedway Organism, by Bruce Covey

The Attention Lesson, by PF Potvin

Navigate, Amelia Earhart's Letters Home, by Rebecca Loudon

Wanton Textiles, by Reb Livingston & Ravi Shankar

notellbooks.org

www.ingramcontent.com/pod-product-compliance
Lightning Source LLC
Chambersburg PA
CBHW030926090426
42737CB00007B/331